# Written
## IN
# HER OWN
# Words

## WISE WOMAN WISDOM

## Compiled by Mary E. Knippel

Best-Selling Author, Book Mentor and CEO and
Founder of YourWritingMentor.com

AUTHENTIC
*grace*
COMMUNICATIONS

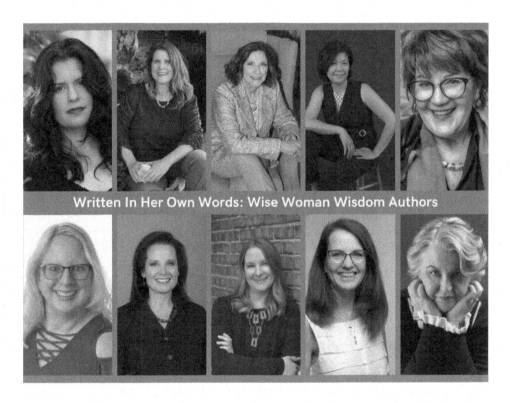

Written In Her Own Words: Wise Woman Wisdom Authors

You can find BONUS gifts and videos from the authors at www.WrittenInHerOwnWordsResources.com.

**DISCLAIMER AND/OR LEGAL NOTICES**

**EARNINGS & INCOME DISCLAIMER**

# DEDICATION

## Special Thanks To:

I dedicate this book to all the women who will see themselves in the words on these pages.

A special thank you goes to the family, friends, coaches, and the many energy workers who have supported our authors through the various stages of their writing journeys. And a special acknowledgement goes to all of our authors who tapped into their inner knowing to summon the courage to share their incredible transformational stories.

# Table of Contents

# INTRODUCTION

It breaks my heart when women tell me they don't have a story. And for those who do acknowledge their story, if by some miracle they have the cheek to harbor a longing to share it, they predominantly wonder who would even be interested in hearing it.

I've been there. It's scary to be vulnerable and transparent on the page.

I understand how those women feel. I've been one of them since I started keeping a journal at the age of 11. Everything I've published personally and professionally started in my journal. The content is vast and contains my hopes and dreams, future plans, unfinished arguments with others (and myself), memories, and processing of life experiences. In other words, my journals hold the specifics for every transformational story I've ever experienced.

My mission is to help women recognize their stories matter. And no one can tell their individual stories from their perspective except for the women themselves.

The transformational stories within these pages offer insight into how our authors have coped with a diversity of life experiences. What they all have in common is their incredible inner strength and deep commitment to being their wonderful, unique, authentic selves.

How does a woman tap into her maternal feelings if she has never been exposed to the behavior, never experienced a mother's care and love, never had the opportunity to fully develop that unique bond between mother and child before it was abruptly severed?

How does a woman create a sense of security within herself if her roots were planted on a foundation of fear and abandonment? How, if she never felt free to express her true feelings? How, if she never felt as if she had choices because everyone else's welfare was prioritized above her own life?

It has been my honor and privilege to be the first reader of these transformational stories. I especially love how the themes of self-esteem, resilience, self-care, and authenticity weave in and out of each story. The resulting cumulative wisdom of this collaborative effort speaks to the compassion and caring that has gone into the telling of these stories and beautifully reflects how our authors live their lives.

What about the wisdom of your story?

What about the transformational story that changed the trajectory of your life?

I would like to remind you that your story matters. It is my firm belief that when we do not share our stories, someone else will not live out the life for which they are designed. Your individual story contains a critical piece of information, a vital part of their story. And if you don't speak up, someone else will not be able to access the story they are meant to live.

Does that sound like it's "out there?" What if I asked you to think about a beautiful tapestry. You know, the kind that has millions of threads and depicts a landscape scene. What if there were threads missing and the picture was incomplete? That's what your story represents in the universal picture.

As you read the transformational stories on these pages, please consider the story you are here to share.

Your story matters. Someone is waiting to hear your story.

# CHAPTER 1

# I Love You So Very Much

## By Dr. Amba Tobin

When I was younger, I forced myself to feel good. I struggled with Self-Love back then. I still do. I think many of us do. I can tell you all the things that are wrong with me so much more easily than the opposite. I teach my clients that all the journaling and all the work we do comes down to one thing. If we can love ourselves, then we can be healed. Yet, for most of us it is a practice. It is not perfection.

I remember in high school I tried out for the All-State Choir. I was an Alto, and I went in to audition with my group: Soprano, Tenor, Bass, and me. I was half-asleep, as it was a Saturday, and I was a teenager. We went in at 8:00 in the morning and sang at 8:30, and then we had to wait around for call backs. My group got called back. They asked us to sing again. Then we were done, as far as I was concerned. If anyone in our group made it, we would hear about it later.

I went home, jumped back into bed, and went to sleep. My mother woke me up with the news that Julie, the soprano in our group, had just called. I had been accepted into the All-State Choir! I was the only student from our high school who had been accepted. Up until that point, I never knew that I was an above-average singer!

I had sung in church since I was 5 years old. And like many others, I had performed a solo of *This Little Light of Mine, I'm Gonna Let It Shine*. I sang in Bible studies and church youth groups. I loved harmonizing, and the others in my Lutheran church group also loved to harmonize. It was fun. It was a spiritual high. Music and art are spiritual.

Whenever I was singing to, with, and for God, I felt worthy.

In 1985, I graduated from high school in Des Moines, Iowa. At that point, I decided I wanted to sing on stages across Europe. I visualized it, and it became my reality for nine years. It was an experience of rolling waves of places, people, music, and love. Over a span of nine years, I sang in the Netherlands, France, Belgium, England, Germany, Switzerland, Turkey, Spain, Denmark, Sweden, and Norway. It was from singing that I felt my self-worth.

I wish we had cell phones back then. I could have saved more photo memories than I did with regular cameras. I do have a small collection of photos of people and places from that time in my life. I am still friends with some of those people who are also on Facebook. It is not the same. Some people, like Madeline Peyroux and Charlie Hunter, became so well known in the jazz circuit that they were able to make a decent living from their music. Some moved back (or moved for the first time) to the States from Europe, and have since sustained an income, more or less, providing for their families through their musical talents.

For me, singing was never as good as it was in Europe. At least, up until now I have not made as much money as I had in Europe. I have not ever felt as well treated here as I was as a singer in Europe. When I was in Europe, I was shifting others' vibrations and helping them feel good. Was it that they treated me like a queen? Or was it that I actually felt like a queen, and they treated me as I felt?

One Christmas, we had a two-week gig at a place called Oba Oba in Ventamilla, Italy. It was very close to the border of the South of France, the Cote d'Azur. I remember my father had traveled to Europe when I was young. He brought home a poster with some sail boats in a marina, and it said COTE D'AZUR. I had dreamed of going there one day---and every year for 9 years, I worked there in Nice, Cannes, and the area, singing the songs of Billie Holiday, Ella Fitzgerald, Big Mama Thornton, Carmen McRae, and one of my favorites, Betty Carter.

Betty Carter was known for being a really challenging band director. She was a unique improvisational singer and piano player, and she would work her (usually very young) band extremely hard. I remember many of the musicians I played with back then were very young and very talented, myself included. Yet, I never considered myself a musician. I felt like being a singer was something different.

When my mom died in 1996, it pushed me into a dark despair. I married my first husband, who did not speak English. He was a co-worker at Max's Opera Café in San Francisco. I was in love with his large family. His sisters and their kids were wonderful. I had missed out on having a big, loving family, and I wanted them as my own. I am still friends with them all, though not with him.

But he did give me two beautiful daughters. For the most part, I gave up singing when I became a mother. A babysitter cost more than I could make in San Francisco as a singer.

When I finally received a small inheritance from my mother, I recorded a CD with one daughter in my belly and another who was just a baby. I also went to visit my friends in Europe and celebrated my oldest daughter's first birthday in the Vondelpark in Amsterdam.

My CD was recorded with some really wonderful heavies: Scott Amendola on drums, Michael Bluestein on piano, Todd Sickafoose on bass, Eric Crystal on sax, and Alex Candelaria on guitar. I made the CD in 4 hours. They were all amazing. I was not as wonderful as I would have liked to be, but it was done. It was called *Miss Henry Sings Angel Eyes*.

A friend had taken a photo of me from the Eiffel Tower, and I chose it to be the cover photo on the CD. The last song, called *Body and Soul*, was recorded 5 years earlier in Amsterdam.

I still think about how I was treated like a queen when I sang in Europe. Something about my singing made me feel worthy, and above others. I felt special, unique, and talented like no other. Back then, I had a sense of self-love that I have not ever felt since. Yet, it was dependent upon others appreciating me for what I could do. It was only because they saw me as something special that they treated me like I was valuable. I felt like a star. People could really see me for me, hear me for who I was.

Sometimes I need approval from others to feel worthy of my own love. Sometimes I can just be there, in my stillness. Or in my song. Or in my work. My self-love is always easier to find if I am looking for it. Or listening for it. But sometimes, I feel the need to surround myself with others who are supportive.

Clients I have seen over the years with cancer, PTSD, kidney disease, strokes, high blood pressure, infertility, and more have faced similar challenges. The root of the problem always comes down to self-love. The work that I do transforms my clients. But it also reshapes my own life, slowly changing me from a person who let life throw me around into a person who uses tools and my education to drive my life consciously and intentionally to where I want to be.

There are many teachers of manifestation, or wellness, or coaches who will encourage us to feel good at all costs. One of them, Abraham, says, "Nothing is more important than that I feel good."

I have a little bit of a problem with this, but let me finish what Abraham goes on to say.

Through Ester Hicks, Abraham says: "Whenever you are feeling less than good, if you will stop and say, 'Nothing is more important than that I feel good. I want to find a reason now to feel good.' Then you will find an improved thought."

Abraham continues by saying, "Anytime you feel a negative emotion, you are in the mode of resisting something that you want, and that resistance takes its toll on you. It takes its toll on your physical body, and on the amount of wonderful things that you are allowing to come into your experience."

I agree that it takes a toll on our physical bodies, yet in traditional Chinese Medical Qigong, we say that it is very important to feel and to honor those feelings of "less than good." Those feelings are trying to tell us something, teach us something, and/or help us grow and evolve. Every challenge is a Gift to Grow and Evolve.

I received one of these "Gifts" recently. It was a concussion.

A week and a cat scan later, I still had the sensation that my skull's nerves and muscles were not quite sure what the heck had happened; they were still responding with swelling and pain. Have you felt immense pain before? Pain means stagnation, specifically stagnation of the energy, or Qi, which usually moves smoothly through an area of the body with grace and ease. Therefore, general health Qigong (pronounced Chi Gong) and sometimes prescription Qigong exercises and meditations are vitally important.

My positive self-talk lessons came into play when I wasn't able to drive safely after the concussion. I couldn't use a computer or sit up without feeling extreme pain after hitting my head on the Smith Machine Weight rack. Just telling this part of the story makes my head hurt. Sometimes, reliving painful experiences makes the pain come back. That is one reason I am not a huge fan of some kinds of talk therapy. One thing we can choose to do, or not, is to honor our emotions and let them go in healthy ways. We can choose to recycle and transmute them through Mother Earth.

Recently, I had a desk full of work to finish and organize. In one weekend, I put most of it into three big boxes and decluttered my office. Then the boxes sat in the living room until I dealt with them from there.

Sometimes, we just need to move things around to make space. The "stuff" still exists, but it's somewhere else. When we experience emotions that are too much to deal with at the time, we put them out of our minds, on the back burners of our awareness and our conscious attention. Those feelings are still there. They must still be dealt with.

Putting negative feelings to the side and looking for "an improved thought" is great if we honor those feelings and where they came from. It is important to categorize them, and to allow those feelings to move or flow out of the physical tissues of the organs in which they sit, rather than stuffing those feelings down. If you just focus on the positive, it's like you're treating the symptom with a pill rather than addressing the problem at the root. It is not in your highest good to ignore that root cause.

Overwhelm requires some self-care and self-love. How does overwhelm affect your physical body?

**Here are the 5 Yin Organs and their associated emotions and virtues. See if you have any of these challenges, and notice where they could be manifesting negatively within your body at this moment.**

1. Spleen - Worry, Overthinking vs. Trust, Openness, Sincerity

12

2. Lungs - Sadness, Grief, Shame, Guilt vs. Courage, Integrity, Dignity

3. Kidneys - Fear, Loneliness vs. Self-Confidence, Inner Strength, Wisdom

4. Liver - Anger, Frustration, Impatience vs. Compassion, Kindness, Patience

5. Heart - Anxiety, Nervousness, Unmet Expectations, and for some people, Despair and Depression vs. Joy (different from Lungs), Tranquility, and Order

**It can depend on the person, but for me, the answer for overwhelm is a combination of:**

- Heart - At times, there is not enough order, and some expectations are not met. There is a bit of anxiety.

- Spleen – Sometimes, problems arise here due to worry, overthinking, and a lack of trust that everything will be okay.

- Liver - Frustration and impatience can add to overwhelm.

There are healing sounds for all the organs (and gray smoke visualization for the Kidneys) which you can use to pull the uncomfortable emotions out of the physical tissues and simultaneously from your mind's thought patterns. They are not easy to demonstrate in writing, but please visit my website for examples.

You can teach yourself how to feel full of order, trust, patience, and compassion rather than simply moving your feelings to the back burner. You can learn to honor and let go of uncomfortable emotions and recharge those virtues that make you feel good. You were born with them. You can learn to go with the natural flow instead of being forced.

If you or anyone you know is ill in any way, either with disease or with emotional dis-ease, here are some journaling questions to try. I often ask myself and my clients to journal on questions relating to those aforementioned Yin organs and their associated emotions:

- When in your life have you not felt trust? Around whom?

- When in your life have you not felt worthy or dignified? Around whom?

- When in your life have you felt lonely or fearful? Around whom?

- When in your life have you felt anger or had your boundaries crossed? Around whom?

- When in your life have you felt that your expectations were not met? Around whom?

With the answers to these questions, next you will ask: Why is that important?

And with the answer to that question, again and again you will ask: Why is that important?

You can go on forever with this single question, and if the answer is not "Because I want to love myself," then you have more journaling to do.

All of my clients have had one thing in common, whether they were diagnosed with cancer or kidney disease or PTSD. They each had a person in their lives who continuously told them there was "something wrong with them." They each had the gift of overcoming that false belief. Through forgiveness work and cultivation of those positive virtues in each of the 5 Yin organ systems, my clients have been able to plant the seeds of self-love.

The events in our lives are all stories. Even smaller than that, they are each one frame within a larger movie. So far, our own frames and stories have brought us to this point, filling a treasure chest with pearls from each of our lessons learned. If we have not yet learned how to love ourselves, the lessons will repeat.

The physical cells in our bodies listen to our words. Words have power. The most important thoughts and words we say to ourselves can change our lives. What are you telling yourself?

Everything comes down to self-love. How do you get to that point at which you truly love yourself?

Well, you learn as many self-care tools as you can, and you surround yourself with supportive and loving and encouraging people.

I teach women how to achieve self-love at all of my many self-care and self-love women's wellness retreats. We hold them every year. Attending a self-care retreat is a very effective way to start honoring and loving yourself right where you are in life, right now. The more tools you have, the healthier you will be. Optimal health is the goal. True wellness comes from self-love, and it shows up as a physically healthy body, a mentally balanced emotional life, a spiritually fulfilling friendship circle, and a spiritual relationship with your Higher Power.

Our goal is to look in the mirror and say, "I love you so very much," and mean it.

In our retreats, one of the exercises we do is our Positive Self-Talk Lesson. Take the time to journal about what each word means to you. Note that 3 and 4 are not the same, but similar.

**Positive Self-Talk Attributes:**

1. JOY

2. ANTICIPATION

3. GRATITUDE

4. APPRECIATION

5. OPENNESS

6. RECEPTIVITY

If you find this exercise to be interesting and helpful, I'd love to see you at my next retreat where we can work together on the next steps of the exercise. **Regardless, do visit my website for some free resources. Let's get to know each other online at www.sitwellness.com/retreats.**

My hope is that today, tomorrow, and every day going forward...you can look at yourself in the mirror and say, "I love you so very much," and mean it.

# About Dr. Amba Tobin

Dr. Amba holds a Doctorate in Medical Qigong Therapy from the International Institute of Medical Qigong. She completed her undergraduate work in Child Development and Psychology at San Francisco State University. Dr. Amba is a yoga instructor from the Bhramananda Ashram. She is also a Level 3 Qigong Instructor, a Food-Based Healing Expert, a Breath Empowerment Workshop Facilitator from the Supreme Science Qigong Foundation, and she has studied Tummo with Wim Hof to learn the Wim Hof Method.

# CHAPTER 2

# God Draws Straight with Crooked Lines

## *By Clare D'Agostino*

Think back on a time in your life that you will never forget. Perhaps it is your wedding day or the birth of your child; maybe it was the death of a loved one or your divorce. I remember my life-changing events as if they happened yesterday; they are imprinted on my heart forever.

The crisp October air filled the car on the silent ride home. After three months of treatment, my 17-year-old daughter was finally coming home. The January day three years before, when she decided to take her own life, seemed like a lifetime ago.

For me, those three months were full of fear and loneliness. Now that we had pulled through and made it to the other side, my mind was racing with endless thoughts. "What do I do now? Where do we go from here?" I glanced toward the passenger seat where she was staring blankly ahead, squeezing her pillow. I saw my little girl suffering, although now there was a glimmer of hope I hadn't seen before.

I turned back to look at the road ahead and thought to myself, "We're finally on the same path." The scent of the season gave me peace; this had always been my favorite time of year. We continued to drive along the road, taking notice of the leaves bursting with bright oranges and yellows, and I breathed it all in.

The road that led us to this autumn day had commenced three years earlier on January 6, 2012. How was I to mother my daughter, who was in so much invisible pain? I felt every ounce of her suffering, and I ached to ask my own mother for advice.

I found myself in survival mode. My daughter had been suffering for her whole life, and I only saw a fraction of it. Her desperate act and the journey that ensued took us on a wild roller coaster ride, for years. My world as I knew it flipped upside down in a matter of seconds, because that's how it happens. Everything changed: school, work, social commitments, and relationships.

"Why do people validate illnesses like cancer, Alzheimer's, and broken bones, but they turn their backs on mental illness?" My daughter asked this question often, and the only explanation I could come up with was fear. People were afraid of what others would think if they found out their friend or loved one was suffering from a sickness of the mind.

Just because you can't see the pain doesn't mean it isn't there.

She was crying out for help in a room where no one noticed. Her diagnosed mental illness was quickly disregarded and easily dismissed by those around us. So, my daughter withdrew from everyone, including me, crawling into herself and heading down a road of self-destruction. Hours and hours after she was admitted to the hospital earlier that morning, I was finally home. It was eerily quiet. No one was talking, as if a thick fog had settled onto our house, erasing all sights and sounds. Personally, I was in the eye of a hurricane, calm at that moment, with the world swirling and crashing all around me.

I looked at my reflection in the mirror and I knew what to do. I had no idea how I would do it; that would come in time. I needed to figure out how to not only support her, but to understand everything she was feeling so I could support her in her fight for justice. I had so much to learn about mental illness and its effects on the entire family. I would do so, one day at a time. All the while I'd be keeping a full-time job and a part-time job, in addition to making sure our youngest daughter didn't fall through the cracks due to being left on her own.

I thought about how my oldest was only 13. When I was 13, I looked up to my mom with all of the admiration and wonder a young girl holds for the mother she loves with all of her heart. My daughter needed me now, more than ever, and I needed my mom now, more than ever.

Then, I remembered that day when I was 14—and my mom was gone in an instant.

It was Wednesday, May 17, 1978, an uneventful morning. My siblings and I finished our breakfast, kissed our mommy goodbye, and went off to school. How could I have known that it would be the last time I saw her smile, the last time I would hear her tell me, "I love you"?

She was usually home from work before we arrived after school, but that day was different. I had a pit in my stomach, thinking to myself that maybe she had stopped at the store or the dry cleaners on her way home. Glancing at my siblings, who were complacently watching TV, I couldn't bring myself to join them; I was too distracted with the churning upset in my stomach. I was truly worried. A conversation ensued in my head, sounding something like this: "She's fine, she just stopped off at the store. Maybe she ran into someone she knew and lost track of time while chatting. It's okay. Don't worry. Nothing wrong could have happened...not to us...not to her."

I wondered...was I the only one who was worried that she wasn't home?

The phone rang a while later. It was my dad, calling from the hospital. His message was simple and straightforward: "Mommy collapsed at work. The ambulance was called and brought her to the hospital. When I got here, she recognized me and she's resting comfortably now. The doctors and nurses are taking very good care of her. She's okay. I'm going to stay here until visiting hours are over, and then I'll come home. Make sure you all eat dinner and finish your homework. Don't worry."

Time passed in a blur until my dad came home. He gathered my 5 brothers, my sister, and me, and told us my mom's condition was serious. She was resting comfortably in a coma, and we would wait and see what tomorrow would bring. It was past our bedtime. In the morning we would go to school, and if her condition changed, he would let us know.

What did all this mean? I had so many questions, but I feared that if I asked them, they would make the situation real. I couldn't bear to think that my source of comfort and security was not at home with us. The warmth in my heart was ablaze whenever I was near her. We were close, and I absolutely loved being by her side. I was just beginning to navigate my teenage years, and I felt an inner strength from her because she always had my back. She understood me, and I wanted to be just like her when I grew up: a lady full of humility, grace, and poise.

Getting ready for bed, my little sister and I talked for a few minutes. I reassured her that everything would be okay tomorrow. Even though I spoke those words, I could barely say them out loud without feeling a huge lump in my throat. I was so careful not to let anyone see my fear. I knew from that moment on I had to be brave.

I heard my father come upstairs to his bedroom and close the door to make some phone calls to our family in California. I don't recall how many he made. What I do remember are bits and pieces of his conversations… "Joey is in the hospital…she collapsed this afternoon, and an ambulance was called. She recognized me when I first arrived to see her, but then slowly she slipped into a coma. This doesn't look good. I called Monsignor to administer Last Rites. What am I going to do? What are we going to do?"

Morning came and my dad reassured us that we would be notified if our mother's condition changed. My carpool pulled up in front of the house. As soon as I got into the car, I pretended nothing was wrong, even though my entire world was falling apart. The very thought of telling anyone would bring tears to my eyes so I firmly held them back, clenching my jaw, not allowing anyone to see that my heart was breaking into a million pieces. I had to be brave. I wanted to be strong.

We gathered in the cafeteria as usual before the bell rang for homeroom. I was only in homeroom long enough to unpack my books, sit at my desk, and get ready for our first lesson when Sister called my name over the PA, asking me to come down to the office. My heart completely sank. I knew this was bad, and at the same time I thought, "God would never take such a young mom away from her family who needs her. She is only 46 years old. I'll say a prayer on my way downstairs." My teacher asked if everything was okay and I think I said it was; I didn't want to start crying in front of everyone. I gathered my books and headed down to the office. While I was signing out, Sister asked if everything was okay. Putting on a brave face, I told her my mom had been rushed to the hospital the prior afternoon. Her quick response: "Oh dear, she'll be fine, she will be okay." I felt a huge sigh of relief. In my naivety, I assumed that if a Dominican Sister could tell me my mom would be fine, then it must be true. After all, she had a more direct line to God than I did, so she had intel that I didn't.

When we all arrived at the hospital, my dad met us in the hallway to prepare us for what we were going to see. "It looks like she's asleep, but she'll know you're here. It might be scary for you to see her hooked up to the machines, but they are helping her breathe. She might not wake up, so talk to her...say a prayer."

We all walked in and stood around her bed. I don't remember anyone speaking out loud, and we stood around her for no more than 5 or 10 minutes. We made our way out into the waiting area. My dad came out a little later. "She's gone. She waited until her children got to see her one final time, then it was time for her to leave us."

Wait a minute...she's gone? It was time? What do I do now? How do I live without her?

We left the hospital and drove home in silence. I wondered what it would feel like if things were normal again. In less than 24 hours, my mother was gone, and I would never again be able to tell her how much I loved her.

None of us talked about losing her. We just moved on.

That's when I became resilient. From that day forward, I knew I had to be strong, and I knew that was how I wanted to be. I took it upon myself to be responsible and grow up fast, to take care of household matters with and for my dad. That day changed the way we looked at life and death, with each of us processing this traumatic event in our own way.

So how do we move on after someone we dearly love has left us? Grief had altered my perspective, even though I never asked for it. My normal routine was taken away from me. Coming home after school now was heartbreaking, because Mommy was no longer there to say hello and ask me how my day had gone at school. The house was colder now, even during the hot summer months; her absence left the house empty and hollow of warmth.

As the days and weeks passed, I continued to be strong, handling the responsibilities that are reserved for mothers. I grew up fast, and in the process, I lost my identity. As a motherless daughter, how would my questions be answered, and who would offer me advice that only a mother could? Where did I fit in as a teenager now? And looking into my future, how would I plan my wedding without her? How would I know how to be a mom? Why did I have to figure this all out without her?

These are questions I've pondered every day since that day in 1978. After college, I became a teacher. I possessed a great desire to nurture and educate the whole child through their early years of elementary school. A lifelong learner, I began taking classes on human development and self-improvement, and continued to learn from the masters.

Remember that car ride home with my daughter in 2015? Even though she was 17, she needed me more than ever. And I needed to be there for her...not as a doctor, nor a therapist, nor a friend. She needed her mom, just like I had when I was her age. At that moment, I knew I would be able to navigate the hoops and red tape of mental health care, and be present to support my daughter. I also knew I would be able to support my younger daughter, so she wouldn't feel left out or forgotten while my attention was directed elsewhere. I felt the strength of my mom helping me pave this new path, and I knew we would get through it, no matter how daunting the challenge.

I turned to my daughter during that car ride, feeling passionate about my newly discovered mission. "I want to help other moms go through what I just went through. I don't know how, I don't know where, and I don't know when I'm going to do it." All I knew was that this calling stirred my soul so deeply, I knew the opportunity would rise at the right time.

What I've discovered is that, regardless of whatever situation we find ourselves in, we hold the inner capacity to figure it out. I have learned how to respond to, and not react to, situations. I now know that I can't control what's happening in the outside world, but I can control how I respond to life's challenges.

My mission now is twofold. First, I am here to support my daughters. Second, I am here to support other moms who are experiencing what I went through. It's vital that you have the tools you'll need when your world is turned upside-down. You'll be able to step back and look at your present situation, pause, and reflect on how you ended up where you are. Only then will you successfully forge your way through to where you want to go and reach a place where your life reflects your heart's desires. As you navigate this tedious path, I want you to know you are not alone.

Today, I assist mothers in transforming their lives, helping them discover how to mother to the best of their capabilities, how to bounce back from life's challenges with resilience and grit, and most importantly, to live with hope.

If you want to learn how to be a good model of resilience for your children, then I invite you to go to my website at www.ClareDagostino.com/resilience and download my free guide, "Six Simple Steps on the Road to Resilience That Will Change Your Life!"

# About Clare D'Agostino

Clare is a heart-centered soul who helps moms grow an unshakeable core of calm, strength, and happiness while they serve as role models of resilience for their children. Since she was a young girl, she's always been a powerful ally to herself and recognized that she has rights and needs that matter. Committed to her own well-being, Clare has spent a lot of time helping her clients build their own resilience with loving intention and grace.

# CHAPTER 3

# Untethered

## *By Eme McAnam*

Eagles remind me that the truth is wiser than I can see. According to Native American culture, eagles are messengers of courage, wisdom, strength, and power. Sometimes I wait for the wise bird to confirm my thoughts, but I know the answer is in me, not in the sky. Intuition is our gift. Nature may punctuate it in unique ways, as the eagle has for me, but we are called to listen to the "still small voice," even when it doesn't seem logical.

*A breath. Wind gusts from the canyon below. Sitting on the edge of the cliff, it is clear that freedom waits beyond this perch. The crown of white bows. Feathers across the breast of the eagle expand. And retract. Expand. Retract. The raptor moves. Yellow beak lifts as its huge wings open. It reaches for the sky, taking in a full taste of joy.*

I woke. This dream had visited me for months as my spirit tried to reconcile the chaos at work. It was becoming difficult to maintain my integrity as my corporate office compromised essential standards. The vision of the eagle continued to wake me with its message of freedom. Income kept me tied. Dedication held me.

For years, I had envisioned an extraordinary experience for seniors. It was thrilling to see that vision come to fruition. As the administrator of an assisted living facility, I managed a core management team of eight. I was involved in everything from the appearance of the property to restaurant operations, marketing programs, and care conferences. We had a great team. But ultimately, the reports that landed on my desk showed that healthcare was failing. The greater issue was out of my managing control, yet the rest of the operation was impacted by the failures in that area. The entire business would lose its reputation if the problem continued unchecked. Corporate was in denial. I couldn't keep compensating for those shortfalls.

Wandering along River Road in the chilly rain with tears burning down my cheeks, I tried to accept that I could no longer enable the company to do the wrong thing. My over-performance couldn't compensate for the errors that were consistently made under their watch. Branches rustled ahead. My ruminations were interrupted by a huge bald eagle flying from an oak. Shocked, I recognized this punctuation for my thoughts. I heard the words "let go." Yet, it was only in my mind. Maybe it was my heart. Either way, I knew the message was for me to leave. It didn't make sense, but I knew my time at the assisted living facility was done.

Finally, I gave my notice and ensured the operations were tooled to carry forward without a glitch. The moment came. I turned off the lamp on my desk for the last time. As I made my way down the hallway to the garage, tears blurred the gold and burgundy carpet that had cushioned my stride thousands of times. In many ways that work was my joy, my mission. With no safety net, I walked away from nearly ten years of dedication. No severance package. No unemployment insurance. I had only my integrity to lean on.

Euphoria hit as I drove away. It was a huge relief to live my truth without pushing against the wall of the corporate office. That feeling lasted for a few weeks. Cruel realities hit over the next couple of months, though. Bills were still coming in and my efforts to find work were an investment in faith. Networking for two years, I took people to lunch, joined organizations, interviewed for jobs, and spent thousands of dollars before I accepted the truth. Though I had a record of creating successful operations, only the poorly-managed places were interested in a woman who was not young. I couldn't make that mistake again. I'd already learned what that experience did to my life. A vibrant 59-year-old was put out to pasture.

But my dream! The eagle. Why had it brought me to a dead end? I thought I was to jump—and I did. But no one caught me. Somehow though, I was beginning to fly beyond my limitations. I believed there was a reason I was encouraged to leave. Now I was starting to see the freedom was mine to enjoy.

At that time, I'd been single for thirty years. After my divorce, I chose to focus on my five-year-old boy and spend my energy on creating our little family. I enjoyed dating, but never found my one and only. My travel options had been limited as I waited for him. It was too expensive to do much when I was running a household on one income. I never found my personal travel buddy.

Realizing that home ownership was a series of unexpected expenses, I sat on the glider chair in my back yard, contemplating options. I loved my beautiful neighborhood near the river: tree-lined streets with darling bungalows and beautiful gardens, not far from the theater and coffee shop. Yet, my four-bedroom house was more than I needed. Budget was a consideration. Resting my head against the chair as pros and cons crossed my mind, I noticed an eagle soaring above. My sign. I decided to sell my lovely 1928 soft pink stucco home with its hardwood floors and vintage details. My son had moved out earlier to start raising his own family. I no longer needed to stay in the life I had worked so hard to build for us. This was my moment to jump from the story that no longer fit.

Excited to shake things up, I chose an artist loft for my next step. The one I selected was under construction, so I needed a swing plan until it was ready. As I pondered interim options, my son said, "Why don't you travel? Find out who you want to be and where you want to live." Yes! I sold my pretty grey car and purchased a bright red Mazda CX5. Belongings were stored in a POD. My SUV held clothing for various weather conditions. My easel and paints. Canvases. Notebooks. Computer. My French press coffee pot, grinder, and electric kettle.

Aspen, Colorado was my first destination. I'd always wanted to see the Rocky Mountains. The trip along the open roads freshened my mind. I sang along to oldies blaring on the CD player. Rainstorms hundreds of miles away textured the horizon as clouds nearby painted the sky. Wind rushed through my open car windows. Old ideas blew around, ready to be released. A new me was emerging. I was free.

In the distance I saw the mountains. Never have I been so moved by nature. Tears flowed down my face the first time I drove into Glenwood Canyon on Highway I-70. My breath stopped. Car slowed. A beep from behind reminded me that I couldn't just savor the beauty. I needed to move through and take it in as best I could. Tall craggy rock walls pressed close to the road. The Colorado River crashed along the other side. As I continued beyond the canyon, the road opened to mountains far and near. The shapes. The colors. The dance of clouds amidst the new terrain. Enchanting.

I landed in Snowmass Village where I stayed in a one-bedroom Airbnb nestled in a complex next to the ski hill. Setting up my coffee maker and easel, I started to feel at home. My next step was to get a pretty bouquet of flowers. Then I settled.

A stranger to high altitude, it took a few days for me to acclimate, but bliss moved in as I was finally able to walk the mountains. One of my early ventures I hiked with a woman who said she'd take me on a real hike, but I needed to get proper supplies. New boots and a hydration backpack later, she took me to Maroon Bells. It became my favorite mountain range.

My friend and I went out together a few more times, but it was more peaceful to move at my own pace and listen to the trees. The aspens were just turning gold. Air was crisp. Few were on the trails. I'll never forget the day I stopped on an incline and turned to take in the view. Puffy clouds kissed the hills. Aspens appeared as yellow ribbons trailing down the mountains. My body trembled. Nature's beauty was overwhelming. The magnificence flowed into me. It was orgasmic as my body melded with the earth. My eyes filled. Awe moved me. This 'awakening' shook me to my core. Images that had held me together dropped away. Those aspects can be part of me, but they are not who I am. They are things I do. I'm much more than that. Many times, I returned to that place looking for the blissful experience, but my spirit wasn't blessed with that intensity again. Beauty is a reminder of that connection.

After that, I quit waiting for the man of my dreams to show up. Rather, I stayed open to all people and found great healing from touching the lives of others and letting them touch mine. People appeared from various places along the way. Hiking. Shopping. Twelve-step meetings. I visited with strangers and found we're alike in more ways than I'd imagined.

I explored art in my quiet hours. Writing, painting, and photography kept me entertained. Having been a singer/songwriter in my youth, words came easily, but prose falls onto the page in a different way than songs. A new version of me blossomed: the novelist.

The year flew by quickly. It was difficult to leave the freedom of the road, but it was time to settle. I moved into my artist loft. Twenty-six-foot ceilings towered above cement floors. HVAC and sprinklers were visible. Huge windows overlooked the Mississippi River. It was so unlike my former cozy home, but beautiful in a different way. My year taught me that home is where I land. Emptiness stepped aside as a huge eagle soared on the thermals outside my window. I felt welcomed.

That chapter on the road leading to my life in the artist loft gave me permission to surrender to whatever muse appeared. My first major adventure was a weekend performance of a song I had written as my son was leaving for college. *Fly Away* became a performance event at which I sang and pontificated about the transitions of life for eighteen hours over three days. I sculpted an 8-by-10-foot mountain out of Styrofoam and painted it. Grapevine, which I wove into a 6-by-8-foot nest, leaned against it. I performed there, dressed as an eagle woman in a hat I fashioned myself. It was thrilling to own my artistic nature!

Covid slowed life down. I couldn't do more performances or photography shows. Instead, I got serious about writing. *Freefalling, A Novel of Senior Romance*, is the gift of that time. It's the story of a successful sixty-year-old woman seeking love. She enjoys her happiest years, even as dementia creeps into her life. My book will be released in 2023.

Full circle happened. An owner of the company I had left ten years earlier suddenly passed away. For some reason I was compelled to go to the memorial. It had been a long time since I had split ties, carrying the pain of that experience. It was time to close the chapter. To my surprise, people were thrilled to see me. Two of the worst perpetrators told me they had learned my assertions were correct. They apologized for how they had treated me. I was grateful for their words, even though my heart had forgiven them years before as I walked the mountains.

Looking over the ten years, I see a pattern. My suffering comes from the belief that I know what's good for me. When that doesn't happen, I resist. Yet, when I surrender to that voice inside, life works itself out. My loss of employment, subsequent fears, and ultimate surrender created my most treasured year, which led to my creative life. Happiness I couldn't have anticipated came from being untethered and surrendering to the unknown. Freedom. I realized I need to stay out of my way for the miracles to happen. I'll keep listening...and waiting for eagles.

I'm blessed. My son and his family have returned to my city. Walking around the lake near his home, I saw a bald eagle perched in the tree. Yes, I thought. This is good. A few days later, my son mentioned that he and his wife had seen it too. I'm not sure he feels the same magic in the presence of eagles, but he did take a picture to share. That's a start!

Are you ready to enjoy more freedom? Inspired to listen to your own intuition? Willing to surrender? I invite you to download three complimentary professional photographs from my collection. They are on my website. Go to www.EmeSpirit.com/untethered to see them, and to view my other creative works. They are my gift to you, with these words as reminders:

**Listen** to the "still small voice," intuition.

**Surrender** to the unknown.

**Freedom** is ours to enjoy, even if it's only a walk in the woods.

# About Eme McAnam

Eme lives in Minneapolis, MN as an artist. Currently, she's a photographer and author of *Freefalling, a Novel of Senior Romance.* Her novel is expected to be released early next year. She's a proud mother to her son and his wife, and loves to be Grandma. Eme has always approached life from a creative perspective. Even as a leader in business, she was innovative. Creativity helps her to be spiritual, yet audacious.

# CHAPTER 4

# Overcoming Codependency

## *By Ingrid Dick*

"You are one decision away from a completely different life."

Codependency is a toxic state to be in. It's a constant back-and-forth, in which one person, the "taker," has a desperate and often narcissistic need for attention from the other person, the "giver." It's a state of mental, emotional, physical, and sometimes spiritual dependency on a family member, friend, partner, or even coworker.

This is a topic with which I am intimately familiar. While I am not a psychologist, doctor, or nurse, nor do I work in the mental health field, I draw from my own personal experience as a long-time caregiver and enabler in a codependent relationship with a loved one.

Are you the "giver" like I was, stuck in the endless cycle of dysfunction? Are you part of a dangerous duo, going back and forth, playing an endless game of tag, reacting and

43

responding to a cycle of emotional blackmail and subterfuge in your relationship?

Are you even aware that you are being manipulated, gaslighted, and unwittingly lured into a codependency? For me, it happened so slowly over a long period that by the time I realized what was happening, my circumstances already had a stronghold over me. The relationship had affected my physical and emotional health, and manifested through anxiety, depression, an escalating mood disorder, and dependency on alcohol as a way of self-medicating.

People in my inner circle, as well as friends, colleagues, and extended family members failed to either notice or to call attention to any of this. I was completely unaware of what was happening. While there were a few raised eyebrows and words of encouragement about taking a "time out" and practicing better "self-care," I am certain that no one really knew of the chaos that reigned behind closed doors, or underneath the façade of social media.

I encourage you to examine ALL your relationships to determine if there is any level of codependency, imbalance of power, or transactional nature. Do your interactions with any particular person leave you feeling anxious, confused, insecure, frustrated, depleted of energy, or even angry? Maybe your experience is not to the extent of mine, and I certainly don't want you to go looking for trouble, but it could be something to examine deeper.

What is this dynamic, how does it happen, and what can you do about it? Based on my own intensely personal experience, I will share the recurring behaviors I discovered and watched for, and what I did to overcome my situation.

## The Dark Side of Give and Take

While codependency is not technically a clinical diagnosis, it has been linked to mental illness, including Bipolar 1 and 2, Borderline and Narcissistic Personality Disorders, and even Schizophrenia. Attachment style patterns that are learned and developed in early childhood, along with familial cycles of dysfunction going back generations, are often at the core of these types of relationships.

Codependency has also been linked to addiction, as well as physical and mental abuse. Childhood trauma and abandonment issues are also a trigger for codependency in a relationship. It's often necessary to look at the origins and root causes of the problem, especially if your relationship is with a family member. Key components of codependency are often linked to ancestral influences; we keep repeating the manipulative and subservient behaviors that we witnessed in the generations that came before us.

The "giver" is the codependent part of the couple. The unhealthy dynamic usually starts with the best intentions, innocently and unknowingly. Codependency comes in many different shapes and sizes, but all cases are psychologically destructive and often abusive in combinations of either verbal, mental, emotional, and even physical abuse. Poor self-esteem, a sense of walking on eggshells, and overwhelming guilt makes it incredibly difficult for the "givers" to disengage from such toxic relationships. However, that's what it ultimately takes to put an end to the cycle: the "giver" must firmly maintain physical and emotional separation and total radio silence.

The "taker" is the devious and diabolical engineer of the dysfunctional duo. Here are a few of the scenarios I experienced. These are questions to ask yourself upon reflection and closer evaluation of your relationship:

- Does your "taker" lash out in anger, or have a short fuse?

- Do they become defensive, especially when they feel their control wavering or their lies being exposed?

- Are they gaslighting you, making you question the truth, claiming their recollection of an event or conversation was correct, and yours was wrong or imaginary?

- Do they accuse you of being "crazy" or "stupid" and engage in other name-calling and use of demeaning language?

- Are they critical of you, your talents, and your achievements when their own are lacking or not meeting expectations?

- Do your interactions with them leave you feeling "icky," exhausted, defeated, and on the verge of tears, or perhaps even trigger a bout of ugly crying?

Yet they continue to draw you in with their lies and disingenuous promises to change their attitude and behavior, and you continue to stay and try to "fix" them, as only you can. Your love and commitment to them is so intense that you will do anything to pacify them and to salvage the relationship.

## I Want to Break Free

So, how do you break the cycle? What, if anything, can you do? First, you need to recognize the signs that you are the "giver."

- Are you unable to set healthy boundaries with that person, or find yourself incapable of saying "no" to their unreasonable demands?

- When they say "jump," do you respond with "how high"?

- Do you experience guilt and self-loathing no matter whether you give in to them or oppose them?

- Has your relationship become purely transactional? Do they only reach out or respond to you when they want something?

- Do you deny that their behavior is hurting you?

- Do you think to yourself, "Tomorrow will be better"?

- Have you thought about leaving or ending the relationship but keep putting it off because you are waiting for a "better time"?

Life with my "taker" was exhausting. They were continually acting out: having meltdowns, threatening or engaging in self-harm, destroying property, trashing their room, telling boldfaced lies, and twisting my words around to use them against me in a sinister form of gaslighting.

How did I respond? I gave in to their whims, submitted to their control over my emotions, endured their anger, and accepted that their problems were my fault. I lived in fear of the next death wish, accusation of neglect, and insistence that I drop everything at any given moment to serve their immediate needs.

It became a cycle of love and hate, of guilt and shame. I remained under their spell, continuing to believe their lies. I was convinced that I could save them, even though they continued to make poor life choices that affected their health, dragging everyone in their inner circle down with them.

Chaos reigned, and they left a trail of bruised egos, broken hearts, and shattered dreams in their wake. As the "giver," I believed I was the savior who could turn things around for them and salvage our relationship.

Eventually, after I suffered from two nervous breakdowns and underwent extensive counselling, I started to break away. I began to set boundaries and learned to say "no" to my "taker's" unreasonable demands. I started to release their control over me. I strived to overcome my feelings of inadequacy and disempowerment. I examined every aspect of my life: values, vison, goals, identity, feelings, and unmet needs. Many of these were intricately tied to the reasons why I became entangled in a codependency in the first place.

However, when I finally had the epiphany that I could not fix my "taker's" problems, there was only one solution, my harsh truth. And that was to disengage, to separate myself from them completely. The final straw happened when my "taker" physically assaulted me in a frightening and escalating surge of rage.

## Life After Codependency: Dealing with Disengagement

Turning 50 was a huge moment for me, one that left me feeling excited, curious, and a little bit anxious. This milestone coincided with the height of my codependency. I entered into my new life season alongside the unraveling of my "taker's" psyche and their own struggle with mental illness and substance abuse. My latest transformation journey led to a significant life-altering upheaval that left those close to me reeling. Walking away from codependency, embracing my newly found freedom, and exploring my identity beyond family life and child rearing has been both empowering and heartbreaking.

This was not a decision I took lightly. I worked on it with the support of my therapist and psychiatrist, as well as my beloved friends, many of whom have experienced the same types of relationships. I tapped into support groups and connected with others whose stories mirrored mine. They all helped me to accept accountability for my role in the relationship, giving me the courage to walk away and embrace an unknown and unplanned-for future.

Now, I am in a place of peace instead of turmoil, clarity instead of confusion, and unconditional love instead of jealousy, gaslighting, and manipulation. I set clear boundaries for myself when it comes to building new relationships or continuing to nurture current ones. My requirements are simple: I am seeking emotional maturity, radical honesty, and mutual love and respect. Gone are the days when I would tolerate transactional, superficial, or insincere relationships. I will continue to work on extreme self-care, and I will be unafraid to ask for help.

I took an interminable and painful road to get to my current destination. I share my struggles, challenges, and insights, along with my successes and achievements, in the hope that my story resonates with you. May it motivate you to make that one decision that will change the trajectory of your life.

Please understand that you are not alone in your state of overwhelm and confusion. Change is scary. But in my experience, staying the same is scarier. One of my greatest lessons from this experience is that it's okay to not be okay. Take it one step, one day at a time. Ask for help, lean on friends and family.

You can choose to stay where you are, remain uncomfortable, live in denial, waiting for the "right time" to make a change. Ultimately, settling for less than you deserve will only prevent you from experiencing true happiness. This is true no matter what your situation is: a codependent or stagnant relationship, an unsatisfying or dead-end job, or a series of escalating health challenges.

You are one decision away from a completely different life. Be aware that choosing to do nothing is also a decision. What will yours be?

As an Integrative Health and Nutrition Coach (they call me Coach Ingrid, The Green Goddess, OR The Diabetes Diva—I respond to all), I work with my clients on mindset, reframing, goal setting, and developing realistic and timely strategies for making life changes that will heal them physically and emotionally. I motivate and encourage others to empower themselves, to make their health a priority and restore their life balance. This is the motivation for including my story amongst the wise words of other women who have also undergone incredible transformations, and for whom I have the utmost respect.

Whether you are someone who is recognizably experiencing a codependency, or you want to tackle your fears, doubts, and limiting beliefs so that you can create the future you ultimately desire...reaching out to me may provide the lifeline you are seeking!

Here are a few insights that I've gained along this very difficult journey. Please note that the reason I have kept my loved one's name and the nature of our relationship private is because we are both still on the path to reconciliation and healing, and I want to protect our process. But I felt compelled to share my experiences and feelings so I can let go of the past, learn from my own shortcomings, forge ahead towards a happier and healthier future, and pass on my wisdom to whomever needs to hear these words.

## Coach Ingrid's Top 5 Tips for Navigating Codependency

5. Practice radical honesty. Be accountable for your role in the relationship. Be realistic about the changes that need to happen in order for you to be free of codependency. Stop

those unproductive thoughts and focus on making positive changes.

4. Stop being a "people-pleaser." Question whether your self-worth depends on being a "fixer."

3. Reframe: focus on what you can do, vs. what you can't change. You cannot control the words, thoughts, actions, or behaviors of other people. However, you can command your own responses.

2. Be present. Focus on the here and now, and stop living in fear of an imagined future. The past is done; you can't go back and change anything. Revisit it for the purpose of "lessons learned," but don't unpack your bags and live there.

1. Embrace extreme self-care. Take the time to understand the origins of your codependency. Surrender to the reality that some people will never change; they simply don't have the capacity. If leaving isn't an option, seek help. Above all, forgive yourself, and them, for your own peace. Just let go.

Reach out to me if you'd like. I'd love to learn how this chapter affected you. I'd also love to gift you my Wheel of Life worksheet so you can discover where your own imbalances lie. Please visit my website at www.greengoddess.guru to obtain access to the worksheet, as well as my 4-week do-it-yourself online Preparing for Change: Goals, Reframing, Habits, and Accountability program.

# About Ingrid Dick

Ingrid's alter ego is The Diabetes Diva. She is a National Board-Certified Health and Nutrition Coach (NBHWC) and an Ayurveda Wellness Counselor. She is known as The Green Goddess and runs her own Integrative Health and Nutrition Coaching business. She is in her 50s, Fabulous, and just a Little Fucked Up.

# CHAPTER 5

# Unmute Your Voice

## By Laura Ann Garris

There are moments in which the whole trajectory of life changes. In some of these moments, the "experts" do not have our best interest in mind, and the decision of life and death is in our hands.

That April morning, the pain in my pelvis was getting worse. What had been diagnosed by my doctor as ovarian cysts through a pelvic ultrasound just 2 days before was turning into something much more severe. I was now lying on the bathroom floor, vomiting and too weak to move. My monthly flow seemed too much. What in the world was happening to me?

I had come to a point where the only thing I could do was go inward until I reached a place of raw grit, a place where passion, perseverance, purpose, and hope aligned like a super-fuel of intuitive guidance. It is in that place where the divine within aligns with the divine above and miracles conspire to transform our lives.

My raw grit moment happened on April 12, 2007. I had given away my power to my doctor instead of trusting my intuitive hunch and the feeling that something was "not right" in my body.

Throughout the prior week, I could not shake the feeling that I needed to stay close to a hospital. Each time I drove by the local hospital next to my children's school, I felt a sense of peace. Then, as I drove away, I could feel a sense of anxiety building in my body. None of this made sense to my logical mind. So, I ignored all the intuitive insights and abundant divine synchronistic clues. I chose to ignore and suppress my divine inner sovereignty, and it almost cost me my life.

My husband, Ray, just "happened" to be working from home that day, although his normal routine had him travelling three weeks out of every month. Ray is my anchor and the love of my life. After 10 years of marriage, he had taken on more responsibility at work in order to financially provide for me to stay home with our 2 young children. Dropping him off at the airport on those early Monday mornings, our 4-year-old son Jack would see the planes on the tarmac and shout, "Look, there's Daddy's office!"

Coincidently, our children's Montessori preschool was closed for spring break, so our son and 2-year-old daughter,

Ella Rose, were home as well. Ella Rose was a happy, independent, and loving little girl. She and her books went everywhere together. Her big, beautiful blue eyes melted my heart as she fearlessly explored this world with curiosity and ingenuity. She was my precious angel for whom I thanked God every day.

Our 4-year-old son Jack was kind, smart, and very protective of his mama. His face would light up as he shouted out "MOMMY!" and ran into my arms each day when I picked him up from school. He was an "all-in" type of kid, passionate for all he cared about. He loved to be the "man of the house" when my husband was traveling.

Now, lying on the bathroom floor, I couldn't understand what was happening to me. I called my doctor's office and was told, "Go straight to the emergency room. If you don't have anyone to drive you, call an ambulance."

What the hell?

Since I was too weak to walk without fainting, my beloved husband whisked me into his arms and set me in the front seat of our car, complete with a vomit bowl. He quickly buckled our children into their car seats. Staying conscious and alert was my goal; little did I realize that it would take all my willpower and strength to make that happen as I held tightly to the bowl placed on my lap.

I'll never forget my son, so worried, saying, "Mommy, Mommy, are you going to be OK?" I just wasn't strong enough to answer him, but continued vomiting into the bowl.

Then he cried out loud, "Daddy, Daddy, hurry, hurry! Mommy is sick and needs her doctor." I could tell how scared he was, how powerless he was to do anything to help me. I loved that little boy more in that moment than ever before.

As we arrived at the emergency room, they quickly admitted me into a room for tests and another pelvic ultrasound. The doctor announced the verdict: I was 9 weeks pregnant. However, the pregnancy had stayed in my fallopian tubes and ruptured due to my IUD. Emergency surgery was necessary to stop me from bleeding to death.

The whole event was a blur. What? Pregnant? It was just supposed to be cysts. How did this go so wrong? How had I been misdiagnosed? I had 2 beautiful, healthy children. A third child was not in my plans. Suddenly I understood why I had been feeling weak, having such a "heavy" period, and experiencing the deep intuitive feeling that the doctors had improperly diagnosed my condition.

The hospital had a gynecologic surgeon on call that day who happened to be right there on my floor. She had read my charts and immediately cleared the emergency operating room for me. I had lost well over a liter and a half of blood, and I was losing more by the minute. They had to stop the bleeding, or death was imminent.

During these 3+ hours, my husband vulnerably reached out to friends and family near and far for help. They answered his plea and showed up to support us in whatever way they could, including our dear family friends who rushed over to picked up our children as I arrived at the ER. They kept our children for over a week with no questions asked, and they did it with open and loving hearts. My children were safe and loved, a true blessing that I shall forever cherish!

Ultimately, the surgery was successful. The hemorrhaging eventually stopped. I was safe and back in my own hospital room. My heart was grateful to see my husband and dear friend waiting for me, though they were encouraged not to stay long since I needed to rest. When I saw their faces, I knew I was going to be okay; this surgery would not be the end of me.

Later that week, my family brought in my Bible and a few popular magazines (Sunset, People, and Oprah) to keep me company during my 5-day healing process in the hospital. As I lay in bed looking at my assortment of reading material, I gently moved my Bible out of the way so I would not spill or drop anything on it, or so I told myself.

The truth was, I was not prepared to talk to God about what had just happened to me. I was not prepared to shine the light inward to explore why I had not trusted myself or my intuition with the signs that had appeared. How had this "pregnancy" gone so wrong? How close had I come to dying and leaving my 2-year-old daughter and 4-year-old son motherless?

I was just too weak to process all these emotions. I needed blood transfusions and intensive pain medications. Why was this all happening to me? Nothing made sense anymore. I needed answers from God, and NOW! All I could do was let the tears fall. I was alive. Weak, yes. But alive.

The nurse came into my room. She was kind, but formal. "I have a few questions to ask you for our records. Do you have a Living Will?" she asked.

"Yes," I replied. I remembered getting those documents ready recently so our children would be safeguarded in case something happened to my husband and me—way in the future.

"We will need a copy of it for our records as soon as possible," she stated flatly.

"Of course, I'll have my husband bring it on his next visit," I told her, not really believing I was having this conversation at this moment.

The nurse seemed satisfied with my answers and said she would check back with me later.

I sat in my hospital bed, stunned, thinking to myself, "They think I might still die! Just how bad off am I?"

I started to cry. The tears burst forth from deep within my heart and streamed down my face. It was all too much to imagine at this moment. I just wasn't ready to give up my life. I had so much life left deep inside of me. Something deep began to stir.

As I lay in my hospital bed alone, I heard these words: "Don't be afraid of my Word."

The words were clear, firm, and deeply peaceful.

"Who's there?" I asked, looking around the room to see who had slipped in.

"Don't be afraid of my Word."

Again, the words were familiar, loving, and directed to me.

"Don't be afraid of my Word." The gentle statement was followed by a burst of brilliant golden-white light, a vision in my mind's eye, and then it disappeared.

Wait! Don't go. I wanted more insight. I had just asked God for answers "now," a little while earlier, and here He was providing wisdom and miracles.

What did He mean, "Don't be afraid of my Word?" Did He mean that I was not to be afraid of the intuitive insights I received from the Holy Spirit? Or, was He referring to the act of speaking with others about the Word of God? Or...

Speechless, I sat in awe. I felt such a loving peace come over me. I knew I was going to be OK. I had no doubt in my mind this had been a message directly from God to open my heart and mind to a deeper love, to not be afraid of whatever way He may appear in my life by either word, vision, or miracle. Something had been unlocked from the inside out, and my life was never going to be the same.

I felt a deep welling up of the Divine Spirit within me. I started talking intuitively to every nurse and attendant who came into my room. Though I was in a secular hospital, the staff members taking care of me all happened to be Catholic. That was very odd indeed in a Pacific Northwest hospital!

My main nurse came into the room to see me reading my Bible. I looked up and shared with her my favorite verses, Romans 5:3-5: "Not only that, but we rejoice in our sufferings, knowing that suffering produces endurance, and endurance produces character, and character produces hope, and hope does not disappoint us, because God's love has been poured into our hearts through the Holy Spirit that has been given to us."

The nurse exclaimed that she loved that verse. She was Catholic, and she had truly felt called to become a nurse. She took her faith seriously and it meant a great deal that I shared this scripture with her.

I was amazed at the openness and vulnerability this nurse demonstrated in sharing her faith with me and how easily we were able to talk to one another.

Later, another nighttime nurse popped into the room to make sure my medicine drip was being administered properly. She was having a hard time getting the flow and the new IV going correctly. It was the perfect moment to share that I was so happy to be alive, that now I was soaking up these Holy words in new ways.

She listened intently as she finished with my pain meds and IV, then left the room. As she was leaving, I felt surrounded by love and embraced by grace.

I continued to reach out with kindness to every person who entered my room, sharing words of faith, the miracle story of being alive after this surgery, and the magical synchronicity provided through people and circumstances in divine timing so I could survive this ordeal. I felt that my voice had finally been "unmuted." I felt free to speak my truth with love and courage. It was divine transformation that had miraculously released my self-sabotaged existence and opened me up for divine inspiration to flow through me with confidence. Unmuting my voice allowed me to be the fully authentic self that God made me to be, and put an end to my tendency to hide by playing small.

Later, I shared my experience with many of my friends at my preschool moms' group as we sat surrounded by our active toddlers in our weekly meeting. They were amazed at the divine chain of synchronicity that had saved my life. It was a miracle. They assured me that God was not finished with me yet, and He must have big plans for my life. Now, I just had to stay unmuted to divine inspiration and keep my heart open.

I did make a full recovery, and I have watched my children grow up to be fine young adults. My authentic voice is now unmuted and full of grit as I stand in my own inner sovereignty. I have been able to go forth and mentor hundreds of girls and women through community programs including Girl Scouts, teaching kids' yoga, and as a Co-Director of a private primary school.

I have rarely spoken of this life-changing event after 2007. However, I recently felt the presence of the Divine Spirit building up in me, inspiring me to share this story in 2022 with a group of work colleagues from various backgrounds. So, I shared the story of "unmute your voice" and the lessons it taught me, how it allowed me to spiral upward in confidence, abundance, and inner sovereignty as I learned to speak authentically without fear or attachment. The hiding game was done. The "playing small" charade was over. Now was the time to share, teach, and coach others.

Today, I call myself the Life Refresh Coach, which means I help women embrace their vulnerability with faith, honor, and intrepid compassion in hopes of unmuting their intuitive voices. I provide encouragement, accountability, and upward-spiraling tools to help them step into the life they love, feeling refreshed, unmuted, and confident.

If you want to learn how to unmute your intuitive voice and stand refreshed in your own inner sovereignty, if you want to stop hiding and playing small, or if you know someone who does, I invite you to visit www.UnmuteYourVoice.net to take my FREE quiz to find your *#1 Challenge to Living the Sweet Life.* You can also apply for individual coaching sessions or attend an upcoming Refreshed Living Retreat.

# About Laura Ann Garris

A woman of true grit, Laura has been able to take the broken, jagged edges of her life from a near-death experience and craft a beautiful, sacred stained-glass window into her soul. She has rebuilt her life one piece at a time by leaning into chards of faith. Never giving up on her dreams, she coaches women to reflect on who they are and what unique gifts they bring to the world.

# CHAPTER 6

# One Good Girl's Story

## *By Mary E. Knippel*

I celebrated my 30th birthday as a college freshman in a drafty lecture hall filled with boisterous 18- and 19-year-olds. It was a momentous occasion for me. I was embarking on an exciting chapter of my life as a college student. It was to be the beginning of me making choices that seemed totally out of character for my "good girl" self. At least that's what my family and some of my friends told me at the time. They didn't understand how I could leave a good job just to take college classes, let alone sign up for an entire quarter in London!

That's what I did, and I loved it!

Looking back, I'd have to call it my summer of discontent. It was the '80s and, although I worked in the tech industry, I was nothing like the professional women wearing pinstriped power suits with shoulder pads on TV. I was a secretary with the usual secretarial duties of typing, filing, arranging travel for my employers and, most importantly, never forgetting to keep the candy jar stocked.

It was totally out of the blue when I announced that I was quitting. Everyone was shocked. My family, my friends, and especially everyone at work thought I was happy in my current situation. After all, I had an ever-so-lovely secretarial job. But there I was, giving it up to attend college classes full-time and pursue a 4-year degree.

Why would a mature 30-year-old woman want to go to classes with 18-year-olds? What was going on with her?

I had a husband with a good job. He was a college graduate, I might add. And it had always been my dream to go to college as well. We lived in a comfortable split-level starter home in a nice, quiet Minneapolis suburb.

It was about time for us to start a family to fill that little home. Yes, my biological clock was ticking, and other family members who had not been married as long as we had already had six children between them.

So, what was wrong with us?

Hence, my discontentment.

I'd always known I wanted to be a mother.

I just didn't know that I'd have to prove myself before I'd be granted that status.

I never made waves or disagreed. I was always the "good girl" growing up, the oldest girl in between the boys, with three younger sisters. I did what was asked of me as a farmer's daughter: gathering eggs, feeding the chickens, washing dishes, dusting the furniture, and occasionally watching my little sisters.

I wasn't an outstanding student. When it came time to write a social studies paper about what I wanted to do when I grew up, my choices were not received with much enthusiasm or approval. I wrote about being an actress, a dancer, or a writer. My acting credits included several appearances as the Virgin Mary in our Nativity plays, and a dozen lines as the housekeeper in the class play during my junior year. As for a writing career, that option was considered just as unrealistic as my other choices.

Since I wasn't going to be a doctor, a teacher, or even a nurse, neither my teacher nor my mother saw the need to map out a college plan for me.

It was decided that my higher education would consist of a One-Year Secretarial Certificate from the local junior college.

The best thing that came out of that experience was that it eventually led me to meeting my husband. However, that's quite another story and I won't go into that here. I'll just say that it was one blind date that turned out really well. (We're celebrating our 50th wedding anniversary this year!)

And what does my motherhood status have to do with my decision to go to school full-time?

Well, on the surface we seemed like normal, healthy young adults. Infertility tests were inconclusive as to which of us was responsible for our inability to achieve a pregnancy. We did the charts and followed some well-practiced methods in an attempt to conceive. Nothing. Finally, the doctor suggested we put ourselves on the adoption list and, before we knew it, we'd be back in his office with a houseful of children.

Well, word got around the office that we'd applied for adoption, and I was smothered with good wishes and well-meaning stories about how this one adopted a child and then went on to have six children "of their own." I was not about to have one more well-meaning conversation where I had to bite my tongue so I wouldn't spit out the words "Mind your own business! I don't care what your sister's best friend's cousin did to get pregnant."

My "good girl" had reached her breaking point.

I needed a distraction while we waited, and getting my degree was going to keep me occupied for a long, long time. Thankfully, we didn't "need" my income to make the mortgage payment. And we had already agreed that, when we received a placement from the adoption agency, one of us would stay at home full-time for the first year. Of course, I wanted that someone to be me. In the meantime, I would pursue my other dream of studying writing at the college level.

I think my husband was more puzzled than anything when I told him I was quitting work to go to college. He had a good job as a computer programmer, and when he went off to work each day, our "home life" didn't affect him. But I couldn't disengage from our adoption story at work. It followed me around, and everyone in my life felt entitled to weigh in on how I was "dealing with it."

I wanted to be somewhere I could disengage completely from the sympathetic looks and concerned questions about why we didn't have a family yet.

I saw our circumstances as an opportunity to create a new reality for myself. I could rewrite my story. I made the decision to quit work. I made the decision to attend school full-time. I chose where to go to school. I chose what I'd study.

I decided. I chose. I supported my choices by continuing to work as a secretary part-time for the General College on campus.

I turned my disappointment into an opportunity to make another dream a reality.

I had to fight to become a full-time student. My first college freshman application was not accepted. I called the

Admissions Office to ask why. They seemed to find it odd that a 30-year-old woman would want to attend college full-time instead of taking the more convenient Continuing Education night classes.

No thanks, I'd already attended several Continuing Education night classes with very distressing results. My art teacher laughed at my drawing in a beginning charcoal class. And a composition teacher suggested I drop the class before he had to fail me. I got the impression they saw me as a bored housewife who didn't need their expertise, and someone who they could easily dismiss.

So now, with a rejection from the admitting office in a form letter and a suggestion over the phone that I try Continuing Education, my response was, "No. I want the college experience of going to school full-time with other college freshmen!"

The next hurdle was my advisor, a retired newspaper editor, who refused to put me in the journalism track because that meant I'd have to take a class in reporting. Class requirements included going to the courthouse, perhaps sitting in on a trial, and monitoring police dispatch calls. He didn't think this little housewife could handle it. So, he assigned me to the mass communication track. This track consisted of most of the same electives, but without reporting as a requirement.

Little did he know that I have a natural instinct to ask the most interesting questions. And I have a knack for helping people to get their ideas out of their heads and onto the page. Personal profiles are my favorite type of writing. My specialty is exposing a person's passions and discovering why they do what they do. That really lights me up inside! (After graduation, I landed my job as an Editorial Assistant for a weekly newspaper, where my responsibilities included reporting on local community activities and conducting feature interviews—a sweet turn of events.)

Shortly after I began my first year of college, a flyer advertising Spring Quarter in London caught my eye. Anything to do with that city interests me. London is my favorite city in the world, and I was immediately fantasizing about seizing the opportunity. What would it be like to reinvent myself in London as a student?

Of course, there were the practical questions to be addressed: could I afford the tuition, the price of airfare, and what would my husband do without me for three months? As far as the money was concerned, wasn't that what student loans were for? And my husband was a grown man who was capable of doing his own laundry and making his own sandwiches for a little while.

I didn't debate the question any longer. Nor did I seek anyone's permission or advice. I signed on to join the small contingent that took over the Earl's Court Beaver Hotel for that glorious adventure. The program included an in-residence professor from our college, who held class once a week in the breakfast room. The rest of the time we were free to explore London! We attended plays, both alone and with the group. Written reviews and lengthy discussions followed.

By the way, I wasn't the oldest student on this adventure. Our group of 25 students included four women over the age of 21. One was a retired teacher, another was an empty nester, finally finishing her degree, then there was a graduate student (our Teaching Assistant) and myself.

I became the mother of a beautiful daughter the same year I graduated from college. She arrived just as I was beginning my last quarter. As we neared the top of the adoption list, I elected to do Independent Study classes for the spring quarter so that I would be available. My intuition successfully guided me in making that decision, as we got the call to come pick up our baby girl on April 10.

I saw glimpses of a more confident me when I took a chance on going after my dreams and rewrote my story. Do you know what? I found out that I really like her! I allowed her to come to the surface more than just occasionally and, to be honest, it scared me. I was thrilled and terrified at the same time. I was embarking on a journey to discover myself without support or encouragement from friends or family, because they didn't understand the need or the hunger within me.

Yes, I had a perfectly good life.

I wanted something more.

I want something more for you.

Going to London may not thrill you. However, I'll bet you can relate to the juggling act of choices women face as we struggle to create and maintain a work/life balance.

How do you make yourself a priority without feeling guilty? How does a woman weigh the consequences of pleasing herself against the repercussions of displeasing others who have very differing expectations of her?

How does she stay true to herself in a world that wants to entrap her in a story that is no longer hers?

What I'd like you to take away here is that you can rewrite your life. If there is something you long to do, one way to transform that longing into reality is to start journaling about how you could make it happen. Walt Disney didn't dream up Disneyland one day, then build it the next. It took planning and persistence. Rewriting your story and taking center stage in your life means living in the present moment while steering your course toward the adventure that stars you as the leading lady.

Once I made the decisions about college and London, I gained confidence in this version of myself and continued to say yes to choices that empowered me to be the Mary I wanted to be. I felt free to be my authentic self, despite the world's expectations of me.

I continue to rewrite my story and say yes to myself. Sometimes it is an easy response, like self-care in the way of a massage, facial, or mani-pedi. Sometimes it is a balancing act, juggling family commitments and expectations with opportunities to explore my writing and creativity by attending fun workshops with friends.

I recall signing up for a creativity retreat with a very good friend I'd met at the worst writing retreat I'd ever attended. We both say that the best thing that came out of that New Mexico disaster was our friendship. We live on opposite sides of the U.S., and make it a practice to get together at fun workshops each year. We select our workshop locations carefully so as to take turns doing the most traveling.

One year, my friend had to opt out of the retreat at the last minute because of health issues, which meant I had to attend all by myself. I didn't know a soul! It could have been a terrifying experience for shy, quiet Mary; however, Marvelous Mary had an absolutely terrific time.

That particular retreat turned out to be a blessing in disguise. I was forced to spend time with myself, and I also had the opportunity to forge new friendships. Both options were equally enjoyable, and I loved that retreat for the wisdom it brought me.

Over the years, I have attended many workshops, each one focusing on various aspects of writing. I love incorporating hands-on experiences to enhance the stories that connect us. Beads, hand-made paper, rubber stamps, paint, fabric, and even leather have found their way into workshops I've facilitated to help writers in search of their unique stories. I especially love crafting journals and then filling them with my thoughts and dreams.

I believe journaling is key to discovering your authentic self. Dreaming on paper gives your subconscious a way to communicate with your conscious self. Give yourself permission to start a journaling practice of writing longhand for 5-15 minutes every day, and I promise you surprising things will start happening.

Your story matters. No one else can tell your story. You have something exclusively your own to share with the world. Among your many life experiences, there is an incident that changed the trajectory of your life, an event that has contributed significantly to who you are today and how you are impacting the world. That event is the root of your transformational story.

I've created a *Written in Her Own Words–Wise Woman Wisdom Discovery Journal* as a gift for you to discover your transformational story. As a journalist, I often use these familiar prompts to get started writing. You can do that too. I've created writing prompts to use as your writing spark. Download your Discovery Journal at

www.WrittenInHerOwnWordsFreeGift.com.

# About Mary E. Knippel

Mary E. Knippel, Book Mentor, international speaker, best-selling author, and journalist for over 35 years, mentors women to get their transformational stories out of their heads and onto the page as a means of growing their business or leaving a legacy. Sign up to learn how to become an author in the collaboration book series "Written In Her Own Words" and receive writing tips on her website: www.YourWritingMentor.com.

# CHAPTER 7

# Lessons from My Daughter

## *By Rebekah Lara*

I never thought that the day my daughter went into liver failure would end up being such a pivotal and positive moment in my life.

I could tell it would be a moment that I would never forget, but what I had no way of knowing was how it would change me to my core.

I've spent most of my life as a pessimist, believing that I've been a victim.

Maybe you can relate?

Life is full of disappointment, loss, grief, hardships, and pain. It's unfair.

Yet, the most important lesson I've learned, despite it all, is that I'm in control of how I respond to these difficult, challenging, and devastating situations. I get to decide how I will handle these moments and move through them.

It took me 42 years to learn this.

## March 1, 2018

I remember that day so clearly. It was my birthday, and the kids had a day off school. So, it was not a day off for me, but I was happy to be home with my 3 daughters, spending my birthday with them.

The day started off with a parent-teacher conference. My daughter Emmalene's 3rd-grade teacher and I had both noticed that Emmalene was suddenly experiencing new difficulties with her schoolwork. Reading had become a challenge in ways that confused me, her memory seemed "off," and she was struggling with her basic math facts. So, we decided we should meet for a parent-teacher conference and put our heads together to try to figure out what was happening and come up with a plan for supporting Emmalene.

One of our babysitters came over that morning to watch all three girls while I attended the meeting. I took advantage of this opportunity to sneak out to lunch by myself for my birthday. It was a glorious, quiet lunch with just my book and a good cup of coffee. It was a rare treat I gave myself.

Little did I know that it wouldn't turn out to be a memorable day because it was my birthday. It would, however, become the day that my life was turned upside down.

When I arrived back home and relieved the babysitter, I prepared to have a friend of Emmalene's, along with the friend's younger brother, come over while their parents attended their own parent-teacher conferences. The kids were all enjoying this little built-in playdate until Emmalene walked down the stairs and told me she wasn't feeling very well.

I told her to sit on the couch while we figured out what was going on. Before I even had a chance to ask her what was wrong, she ran to the bathroom and got sick.

Emmalene had been 100% fine all day, and I had no idea she didn't feel well. These symptoms seemed to appear out of nowhere.

Over the next 24-48 hours, Emmalene continued to vomit on and off. Along with her inability to keep any food or fluids down, she developed a fever of 102.3 degrees.

By the end of the 3rd day, she was still not able to keep anything in her stomach. We noticed the vomiting had turned into retching, and some flecks of blood were present. Of course, this was a cause for concern, but we stayed by her side and waited for the virus to run its course.

By 8:00 pm that night, my motherly instinct told me something was really wrong. I decided it was time to take her to the emergency room.

As I rushed her to the local ER, my head was spinning. I was confused, worried, and concerned for her. Emmalene had always been such a tough kid, and up until this point she had already been through so much as a child. Her list of surgeries, diagnoses, medications, and therapies is too long to list, and honestly, it is still quite upsetting to me when I see it all listed on one sheet of paper. How much physical distress can one child go through before the age of eight?

By this point in her life, she had already had 2 spinal cord surgeries to repair her tethered spinal cord, including one surgery that required us to fly her across the country. She'd also had to have a gastrostomy feeding tube (often called a G-tube) placed after 7 years of doctor appointments both in and out of state, therapies of all sorts to get her to eat and drink, accommodations at school, and so many attempts at reward charts and every other trick or tip that was thrown our way.

The list goes on, but the most important (and mind-blowing) part of it all is how she handled every appointment, therapy session, and doctor visit with maturity and bravery far beyond her young age. So, seeing her calmly agree that we should go to the emergency room gave me the strength and courage to take her on my own while my husband stayed home with our younger daughters (ages 4 and 5 years old), and the assurance that I was not overreacting. It was indeed time to figure out what was wrong with our daughter.

We arrived at the emergency room around 9:00 p.m. on Saturday, March 3rd. The emergency doctors and nurses promptly began assessing her, ran bloodwork and a urine test, and gave her IV fluids to start. I was glad we were in the emergency room by this point, because she started to take a turn for the worse. Emma started acting a little loopy. She was talking funny, seemed disoriented, and if I didn't know better, I would have said that she seemed intoxicated.

What could possibly be going on with my precious little girl?

The hardest part of this entire journey for Emmalene (and for all our daughters) was all the time I spent alone in hospital rooms waiting, worrying, and having no one to lean on. It's not that my husband wasn't supportive or didn't want to be there. He was always highly supportive, caring, and helpful. Yet, someone had to be home to take care of our younger daughters. Without our parents around to help with our girls, we had to divide and conquer.

So, as usual, I sat by myself, texting updates to Adam and my sisters until finally the test results came back in. The urine test was negative, but the blood work did show that she had low glucose levels.

The treatment seemed simple: Dextrose via IV for the low blood sugar, Zofran for nausea, and finishing the IV fluids since she was dehydrated. The emergency room doctor concluded that the blood in her vomit (and coming out of her G-tube stoma) was due to tiny tears forming in her esophagus from all the retching and vomiting she had been doing for the past 3 days.

After the treatments, Emma perked up a bit, didn't seem so disoriented, and was discharged at 1:00 a.m. After stopping at the pharmacy for more anti-nausea medication on the way home, I thought the worst of it was behind us. I was relieved to finally get Emma into her own bed so she could recover.

Unfortunately, I was gravely mistaken.

After just a few hours of sleep, I woke in a panic at 6 a.m. when I realized that I had missed 3 calls from the emergency room. The next 74 days would rock me to the core and forever change who I was as a woman, a parent, and ultimately even as a business owner.

Emmalene spent 74 days in the hospital, including 28 days in the pediatric intensive care unit.

All the time we thought Emmalene had a stomach virus, she was actually experiencing acute liver failure. Her liver enzymes were so extremely elevated that the first blood test from the night before took hours upon hours to produce final results because the blood specimen had to be diluted multiple times and retested over and over again. No one in the ER knew what was happening in the lab, and we were sent home without even an inkling that something was very, very wrong.

By the time she was rushed back to the emergency room at 9:00 a.m. that morning to retest her liver enzymes (because the doctors thought that surely there must be some error in the first blood test because the liver enzyme numbers were so astronomically high), we were given the difficult news that it was not an error. Her liver enzymes were now even worse, and she was indeed in acute liver failure.

As I sat there in the ER waiting for the plan, waiting to talk to Emmalene's main gastroenterologist at another hospital, waiting for my husband to find someone to take care of our younger daughters so he could come to be with us, I was reeling. My mind was spinning, my life felt like it was being turned upside down, my heart was cracking in half, and I had so many questions.

My world felt like it was caving in on me. As fear coursed through my body, I answered a call from the GI doctor who had been caring for Emma for years. Calling me on a Sunday was uncommon for him, and it was definitely an indication that her situation was grave. He tried to reassure me that having her rushed to the children's hospital (not the hospital at which he worked) was the best course of action, and that they would be better prepared to treat her there.

When we arrived, she was brought into a typical hospital room on the 20th floor, but it quickly became clear that her condition was worsening. She was rushed down to the pediatric intensive care unit (PICU) due to her altered mental state. As the doctors explained, her liver had stopped functioning, and so her level of toxins was increasing and poisoning her body, including her brain.

By 1:00 a.m. on Day 2 of her hospitalization, we were not only informed that she would need a liver transplant, but also that her mental status was critical. She was disoriented, sleepy, and loopy, and she was also extremely irritable, aggressive with the nurses, and had started thrashing her body around and hitting her head.

This was not my calm, polite little girl.

The doctors made the difficult decision at 1:00 a.m. to sedate her, place her into a medically-induced coma, and put her on a ventilator.

Just when I thought I couldn't be more scared for her, I was thrown into a whirlwind of worry, anxiety, and fear as we were sent to the family waiting room while they intubated her. A chaplain came to sit with us. The presence of this chaplain was clearly meant to be supportive, but to us, it was another indication of just how dire her situation was. We thought we were losing our daughter that night.

No one can prepare you for what it's like to almost lose your daughter because all her organs stop working and you realize she is only alive because of the life-saving measures of her PICU doctors, nurses, and all the machines surrounding her, making it difficult to even see the little girl beneath them.

Despite the fear, worry, and pain our family experienced, I was also filled with hope and faith during those 74 days while she was hospitalized. What happened next feels like a true miracle to me.

On Day 5, after praying for days for her to receive a donor's liver (or for the 5% chance of her liver recovering), Emmalene's liver did miraculously recover. She still had a very long road of recovery ahead of her, which ultimately took 3 ½ years, but she had been given the gift of life and our prayers had been answered.

Now, we just had to get the rest of her organs to follow suit. She was still on a ventilator, on daily dialysis for her kidneys, and receiving all her nutrition intravenously. She would remain in the PICU for several more weeks and in the hospital for 69 days following, before being discharged home.

Most days, I wake up feeling so much gratitude for the life we have been given, the second chance to be together as a family. My daughter's near-death experience has truly opened my eyes and my heart to all there is to be grateful for.

Never again will I take for granted waking up each day with a fresh start. Never again will I take for granted the opportunity we've been given to have another day with our daughters. Never again will I take for granted that this is our one life to live and that we get to decide how we want that life to go each and every day.

But it took me quite a while to get to the point where I felt deep gratitude. I was knee-deep in the victim mentality.

Even though she was home with us, she still needed a tremendous amount of care 24 hours per day. I quickly learned how to be her nurse during the day, and then she had overnight nurses who took care of her from 10:00 p.m. to 6:00 a.m., so we had an opportunity to sleep.

Having Emmalene home with us was a true blessing, but we were also faced with the reality that our daily life looked completely different from before. Watching my daughter navigate her days in a wheelchair with an oxygen tank in tow was heartbreaking. It's not the life I wanted for her, and it broke my heart daily to see her miss out on so much of what the other girls her age were doing.

# Lessons from My Daughter

For so long, we were merely surviving, trying to take each day as it came and make it to the end of the day unscathed and no worse than we started out. It took me a couple of years before I was able to fully come out of that darkness, to truly see all that we had to be grateful for and start thriving again.

Emmalene was my teacher through it all. That young lady taught me so much about resilience and what it means to be courageous, strong, and determined. She was truly unstoppable, and slowly over the next 4 years, Emmalene continued to improve—and slowly, so did I.

My perspective started to shift, and I started to see more of the miracle that was unfolding before our eyes each day.

Slowly, I was able to come out of the fog in which I had been living. Slowly, I was able to see the light and stop ruminating in the darkness.

My daughter taught me by example that giving up isn't an option. My daughter taught me that you can be unstoppable, reach for your goals, and if you never give up, you WILL achieve so much. My daughter taught me that it was time to put the dark days behind us, step into the light, and claim all that the universe has planned for us.

I had wasted so many years—honestly, most of my life—wishing and praying for different circumstances, including with Emmalene's medical conditions. In that time, I was the creator of my own suffering. Wishing for a different situation would never help me, but only hold me back.

This was another lightbulb moment for me.

Instead of ruminating over how I wish things could be different, I now know that I have the power over how I respond to each situation in my life. I have the power over my thoughts about these situations, and I have the power to choose new thoughts and feel new feelings.

This is the true power that has revolutionized my life.

My daughter showed me this through her example, and my business coach helped me see the lessons that were gifted to me during this healing journey. This was a game-changer for me, and my life took a dramatic upward turn—even though my daughter was not miraculously better, even though we still have obstacles and challenges to overcome. I now know that I am resilient and I have everything I need inside of me to overcome whatever life has in store for us next.

I am eternally grateful for this breakthrough in my life.

I've discovered the woman I was always meant to be, a woman I am proud of today, a woman my children can look up to, and a woman who is ready to be seen.

I know what true gratitude and joy really are now. I experience them every day, and I am so thankful for the lessons I've received. Through this experience, I know that these results are available to you too.

I now support other busy mom entrepreneurs who have challenging life circumstances so they can build their businesses while working less. This enables them to be caregivers without giving up their own dreams.

**If this story resonates with you and you know that it's your time to thrive, I invite you to connect with me at www.learntothrivenow.com.** There, you will receive my 3-Part Time to Thrive Workshop Series, which includes lessons on: 1) How to Create More Time in Your Schedule, 2) How to Plan Your Week & Prioritize Your Tasks, and 3) How to Stay Accountable to Yourself.

These are the key strategies that have allowed me to sustain my business all these years, and you can too! Having the benefit of working from home while raising your kids or managing life's challenges is an enormous blessing. I'm here for you, whenever you're ready!

# About Rebekah Lara

Rebekah Lara is a Certified Life Coach and creator of the Time to Thrive program, where she helps mom entrepreneurs build their businesses while working less, so they can be caregivers without giving up their own dreams. With two businesses and 3 young daughters with multiple needs, Rebekah has streamlined her own business systems, manages them all WITHOUT the overwhelm, and is passionate about helping other mom entrepreneurs calm the chaos too.

# CHAPTER 8

# Gone in the Night

## By Rita Aguilar

*You put me to sleep one night, and left me before the morning.*
*So much undeserving faith in you, expecting to see you when I woke up.*
*Night after night I prayed I'd wake up with you next to me.*
*Countless mornings later you were gone.*

### -jai

One morning when I was 12, I woke up and my mother was gone. She'd left me and my five siblings in the middle of the night.

"Why did my mother leave me?" She was just gone. "How could she do such a thing that would forever change our lives?"

Our family wasn't your typical family. My father had moved to the U.S. to work, and he was going to send for us all as soon as he was able. We were living in the Philippines.

The day she left, we went through our regular nighttime routine before bedtime. We ate dinner at the same round table, speaking to each other casually about our day and about school. The night was normal, and so ordinary that I can hardly recall specific details that might have stood out as different from other nights.

After dinner we prepared for bed, bathing, brushing our teeth, our hair. All the while, our mother put together our uniforms for school the next morning. She put us all to bed individually, wished us goodnight, turned off the lights, and then joined us in bed. Usually, the younger ones slept on each side of my mom, so they probably did it that night too. But once kids are fast asleep, it's hard to wake them up. It must not have been much of a challenge for her to leave their side and go her separate way.

When we woke up for school the next day, she was gone. It was still a school day, so we got ready for school, not thinking much of her absence. We waited for the driver to take us to school, and from 7 a.m. to 3 p.m. we went about our normal daily routines.

All I knew was school and home.

After school that day, we came home to still no mother. My older sister and our maids took care of us smaller kids for a couple of days, but then at some point, someone decided that they had better call my dad in the U.S. He couldn't come home, but he immediately called my aunt and grandmother to step in.

I realized she might not be coming back when our grandmother and aunt told us to grab our clothes and school supplies, and my younger siblings brought along their special toys. And that was it. That was the last we saw of our home.

It was as if my mother had just disappeared.

Then we were living in our grandmother's house with the same daily routine: waking up, going to school, and going to bed. Kids like to cuddle when they sleep. Usually, they cuddle a parent, like their mother. But instead of their mother, my siblings cuddled with me. I had taken her place, sleeping between my younger siblings—between all my siblings. There were two more rooms available, but we all insisted on sleeping together in the same room and in the same bed.

I remember certain things, like the way she had shown my siblings and me how to brush our teeth and brush our hair. She had also taught me how to crochet, a skill I passed on to my own daughter.

"What made her leave?" I questioned.

I was only twelve when it happened. Twelve years old and barely a freshman in high school, and now I had to be the one to raise my siblings, seeing as I was the oldest. I didn't have time to cry about it, I didn't have time to let it eat me up inside. I had to make sure we made it to school. I had to take note of all the things we needed so I could tell our grandmother. I had to be the one to cradle my younger brother and sister to bed. It often felt like we were just taken in out of obligation. It didn't feel like it came out of a place of love. They just took care of us as a favor for our dad, for their son/brother.

"Wawel's kids" is what they called us. We were referred to as a single unit. We were granted no individuality; it didn't even feel like people bothered to differentiate us from each other. I doubt they bothered to remember our names.

Growing up, I knew mothers cared for and nurtured their children. My own mother's care and nurturing stopped for me at a young age. I stepped into the role of caring for my younger siblings instead. As a result, I didn't think I would want to have children. I wondered if I would be strong enough to be a mother. I didn't want any child to go through what I went through and have questions in their hearts about why and how their mother could leave them.

I kept wanting to put the pieces of my life together, but it was not possible. The pieces had all gotten lost! At a young age, I learned to face life as my situation continually changed. I tried to make better decisions and to choose wisely. I wanted to show my extended family I was not growing up to be like my mother. I was not her! I could have children and I would care for them. I would raise them to have a healthy and meaningful relationship with me. I might not have had a relationship with my own mother, but that didn't mean it wasn't possible for me to have it with my children. I wanted to focus on what I could do differently, rather than what was assumed of me.

I cannot change what has happened in the past. Instead, I can learn and imagine a better version for myself.

I'm not a person who likes to hold grudges. I find that holding onto them often brings more pain and anger than they are worth. I don't hold a grudge against my mother; I don't even hate her for leaving us. But still, there is one question that always comes to mind: How could she do this to us? How could she just abandon her children with no warning?

Losing my mother at a young age made me realize that our lives must go on. Something I looked forward to was that soon enough we would be joining our dad in the U.S. When that day came, my 3 younger siblings had to stay behind. My brother and I had to say goodbye to them until it was their turn to go to the U.S. to live with us.

It was my first time traveling in an airplane, and my first time traveling without an adult. That's right! A 14-year-old and a 13-year-old traveled alone across the Pacific Ocean, without grown-up supervision.

I learned that those bad things were just temporary events in my life. And those experiences made me resilient for what might come in the future.

The experiences continued, as I grew up without a mother and with a father who worked two jobs. My father worked from 7 a.m. until 12 midnight. He was the first one to wake up and the first to leave the house, and he was the last one to get home and go to sleep. I thought living with my father would make me feel less alone in the house. But in the end, it was just the same in terms of company. I still grew up without a parent in proximity. I understand what my father did for us, and I hold no resentment toward him. Someone needed to make sure we had a house to live in and food to eat. Regardless, when I had children, I wanted to make sure that they didn't feel as alone as my siblings and I did while we were growing up.

It wasn't until four years later, when I was working after high school, that my three younger siblings finally came to join us in the U.S. I stepped right into the mother role with them, since my father was so busy.

As I got older, I didn't want to have children. Growing up without a mother and with a barely-present father was hard. I didn't want to take a chance on having a child whose childhood turned out to be the same as mine. When I became pregnant with my firstborn, something changed inside me. I knew I needed to be there for my child. Once you become a mom, something changes. I wanted my children to always be okay, and I was willing to go the extra mile for them.

Bringing my own baby into this world was the real starting point of my life.

I did a lot of soul searching while I was going through my pregnancy. But at some point, it was no longer a decision I was making for myself. I was making this decision for my child, for my daughter. Whatever happened, I was prepared to be there for her. I promised myself I wouldn't make her feel alone; I would make sure she had both parents and that she felt loved. I didn't want her feeling neglected, unloved, or isolated. I didn't want her growing up looking for a parent. I wanted her to know that even when I had to leave for work, I would always come back. I made sure she knew that I was always coming back for her.

When she finally arrived 8 weeks early, my daughter was delivered via c-section. I knew then that my life was forever changed. When it came time to be discharged, she had jaundice and had to stay a few more days. I wanted to be there for her every step of the way. I was discharged to go home, but I refused to leave my daughter. That was the first promise I made to myself. I slept in a recliner for three nights to be with her.

We were both able to go home on Christmas Eve, and she was best Christmas present I've ever received. I wanted to be there for her every step of the way. I think she knew that we would learn from each other, because she was the best baby.

This baby, who carried all my hopes and dreams, was here for me to take care of. My own child needed me when she was hungry. She needed me to change her clothes. She needed me to carry her when she cried. And I was there to do all those things. We grew together. I grew to become the mother I always wanted to be. It was an adventure, having my first child, but it continued when my daughter wished for a sister.

Ah! How could I disappoint her? I had to tell her that if we were to have another child, we had no way of knowing whether it would be a girl or a boy. It was a challenge to have another child. My daughter grew impatient waiting for her sister; she mentioned that she didn't care whether "it's a boy, or a girl, or a cat, or a dog!" She wanted a sibling. So, there I was again, praying, manifesting, and imagining when and how I could make this happen.

After two years of trying, we were blessed with a baby boy who cried all the time. No one and nothing could soothe my boy except breastfeeding. If my daughter represented my hopes and dreams, my son surely made me feel a very different level of motherhood. I prayed for patience and understanding to deal with the constant crying. And with that, I found new strengths and I experienced different ways in which each child needed me. We choose together how we want to grow and live our lives.

Throughout my early motherhood, I found myself comparing myself to my mother all the time. I asked myself if I was making the same mistakes that she did, if I was going down the same road as she had.

I can't control the future. All I want is the best for my children, but I can't protect them from the entire world. As a parent, you know there will be big things happening in their lives, things that you can't control or even witness at times. Their world grows as they do. I'm proud that, despite my lack of a mother, I was able to break the cycle and provide a loving home for my children. But my journey through motherhood isn't over yet. My daughter is grown now, but my son is only fourteen and still growing. As they say, the best is yet to come.

As a woman and an individual, to have control over how I think and how I live my life, and to share the things that life has granted me, feels so much more complete because I get to live it with my loved ones. My happiness comes from watching my children grow up and live their lives under the love and influence of my parenting. It is so satisfying.

The possibilities are endless; I don't have to be what others think of me. My experiences then and now have developed into a character who is resilient and adapts to life's cycles. Did I overcome my childhood dilemmas? I was reminded of them all the time while growing up, and sometimes even today, the holes in my heart that need filling are still there.

Today I make my own decisions. I am no longer soul-searching, but instead I am manifesting and imagining all the best possible ways to live my life together with the family I have created.

Did I receive help for the emotional trauma I went through? To some people, does that even exist? I often ask myself, how do I heal from this? I can't deny what has happened. I choose to be my children's support system and guide them through their dilemmas. I help myself by accepting the emotions I feel from being abandoned as a child and the puzzling memories of growing up without the love and care of a mother.

To those family members who gave us just the necessities, it would have been nice to receive more understanding and less judgement and expectation from them. I can't make people think or act a certain way.

I can choose to think for myself and do things differently. That being said, the way I choose to do things is not for everyone, but if anybody out there reads and understands my story and feels a kinship with how I learned to cope with my life experiences, I hope they find the strength and courage in their hearts to keep going.

You can better yourself by choosing you.

Choose to love yourself.

Your past doesn't determine who you are today; you are who you choose to be. And now, I am the mother I always wanted to be. I can't imagine abandoning my children. Of all twenty years of my daughter's life, of all fourteen years of my son's life, I have made sure that there wasn't a single moment in which either of them felt abandoned by me.

We are given a life, but we get to create our own adventures and make our own paths to continue to live together. I cannot just leave it up to God! God has given me free will, and I am using it to take charge of my life. Growth is an individual journey. It's my story to tell. And it's your story to tell.

# About Rita Aguilar

Rita Aguilar is an immigrant from the Philippines, and she has lived in California since 1987. Rita lives an active lifestyle with her husband, kids, and dog. She has always embraced the beautiful scenery of mountains and beaches in California. Living and growing up in America has given her the opportunity to live the life she has always dreamed of. She loves to share her experiences and attitudes regarding how she defines her own life.

# CHAPTER 9

# The Pivot Point

## By Stacy G. Fisher

Early in my life I made up that I was fat, and I was ashamed of the way I looked. I began dieting as a tween. After struggling with my weight well into my thirties, I made one of the most critical decisions of my life. In April 2003, I underwent laparoscopic duodenal switch surgery, or gastric bypass, and it saved my life—the quality of my life.

Today, I am an attractive, successful, professional woman, a former senior vice president in financial services, and now a career coach. Looking at me now, most people would find it hard to imagine that I was once obese, morbidly obese. I earned my role as senior vice president at my heaviest weight of 350 lbs. At that weight, I received disapproving looks, and in some situations, I experienced women moving away from me as though they might "catch fat" from me. It took a mental toll to keep the noise out of my head and to learn to show up despite it.

Like so many women around me, I have spent more than half of my life on one diet or another to achieve the perfect body, or at least one that was socially acceptable. Americans have a particular obsession with weight, but the fact is, I would not have survived at 350 pounds. I had to lose weight, and lots of it. Since my surgery I have lost over 220 lbs., but the surgery did not cure me, and it was not magic. The process was not an easy one; it did, however, give me the ability to take back my life.

People would often ask me whether I was "born fat." The answer is no.

As a child, I was always average weight, curvy and solidly built. I was only eleven when my body began to change, and I became very self-conscious and awkward.

I was on my first diet by thirteen, consuming only 500 calories a day. By sixteen, I had convinced my mother to take me to a doctor who gave me a vitamin B shot and instructed me to eat a no-carbohydrate diet. My weight dropped from 130 lbs. to 115 lbs. I was running five miles a day and feeling great, but I found it difficult to maintain those eating habits long-term. By the end of the following summer, I was back to 130 and, although I had kept up with the jogging, college was right around the corner. I felt doomed to lose the war.

During college I tried The Rotation-Freedom Diet, where one eats food every other day and, on the alternate day, eats only these chalk-like wafers. It worked while I was on the diet, but again, that is not a way of eating for life. The weight came back. After college, I started my career at Citibank in Chicago on the corporate foreign exchange desk. Working on the trading floor was hectic. I usually skipped breakfast and did not eat lunch until the market closed. This erratic way of eating, on top of my history of dieting and deprivation, only served to further slow my metabolism. During those years I tried OPTIFAST® twice. Both times I lost 75 lbs., only to regain that weight and then some.

In my late twenties, I relocated to Los Angeles and took a job with Wells Fargo. I continued my diet lifestyle, using the Lindora Lean for Life program for several years. Then I tried fen-phen, which was taken off the market. Like so many dieters, I was always successful for a time, but then I would regain the weight plus a few extra pounds. The number on the scale just kept climbing higher and higher as the years passed.

I knew that the constant yo-yo dieting was not doing my body any good. Like so many others who were searching for a lasting solution, I was becoming hopeless and resigned. In November 1999, I moved with the bank from Los Angeles to San Francisco to lead a team that was developing one of the first foreign exchange internet applications. My team consisted of about ten people, and we did roughly two years of work in nine months. I worked round-the-clock until the launch date.

By the time our project launched in June 2000, I was exhausted and my life was out of balance. I had also gained seventy-five more pounds.

Early in the project, I had attempted the weight management program run by Dr. Joan Saxton. It required that I fast, which I found too difficult given the pressure of the project and the need to adjust to a new city. I abandoned the effort. After the launch, I joined Weight Watchers, then I hired a personal trainer with whom I worked three times a week. The experience yielded few lasting results and, with respect to my body, I felt more hopeless and out of control. My genetic predisposition to being fat was the loaded gun. Dieting was how I pulled the trigger.

Every day I struggled with this inner monologue that pressed me to reduce my weight and questioned how I was going to manage my body. Here I was, a smart, successful businesswoman. There were all sorts of challenges I could overcome, but not this one. My body and my body image continued to be a source of tremendous unresolved anger, frustration, and shame. Waking up each morning, my first thought was, "Thank God I woke up today."

As I continued to gain weight, I accepted fewer and fewer invitations. I felt uncomfortable at parties and events. I only went to the business functions I absolutely had to attend. That was it. I would get frustrated just finding something appropriate to wear—let's see, shall it be the navy-blue tent dress or the black one today? I worried about taking up too much space, and that idea was not just in my head. People could be very cruel, as though your extra fat layer would prevent you from hearing their abusive or unkind words.

Once, while shopping for a pair of shoes for a friend's wedding, I asked the young salesgirl whether they had a pair of plain navy-blue pumps with the heel under 2 inches. She replied, "We do not have anything like that. These shoes are more for pretty people." I did not even respond, because what would be the point?

Then, in early 2002, while perusing the newsletter from San Francisco's California Pacific Medical Center, I read about their program with a leading laparoscopic surgeon specializing in surgery for the morbidly obese. But at that point I still thought that I should be able to tackle my weight issues myself. I had bought into the idea that I was fat because I lacked self-control, and having surgery would somehow be cheating. But the idea was planted. Over the next few months, I investigated the duodenal switch surgery. I was ready to take serious action to intervene in the direction of my life.

In June 2002, a friend died at the age of forty-one of a spinal cord tumor. He left behind a wife, two children, and a legacy of contribution to others. At the time of his death, he was deputy director of the U.S. Office of Tribal Justice. He was a warm, intelligent person, committed to contributing to others and being of service. A vital, productive human being, he was so alive—then gone so quickly. It was shocking.

Just two months later, in September 2002, my cousin's 16-year-old son died suddenly. The day started out like any other. He came home from school on the bus and his mom had taken the two younger children to the dentist. Zack was supposed to stay home, but he decided to drive over to a local hang to meet with his friends. It was pouring rain, and they lived down a winding country road. Zack was speeding. He wasn't wearing his seatbelt and took a turn too fast. The car flipped, hit a telephone pole, and Zack was killed instantly. Emotionally overwhelming doesn't begin to describe what it was like watching my cousin Greg and his wife, Kathy, bury their oldest child. Flooded with thoughts and emotions, I remember thinking that I had no business wasting a day. I wanted to live.

I was ready to commit to living my life. In November 2002, I took the first step and went to a meeting at Pacific Laparoscopy. I completed the steps to qualify for the surgery and was scheduled for April. I could not have begun to imagine how profoundly my life was about to change.

I thought it best to tell only a few trusted people about my decision to have the surgery. I told both my sisters and their husbands, and my close friends and colleagues. I am a guarded and private person. I did not want to hear opinions from people who were not going to fully support me in my decision, or family members who might worry. I needed to be supported by thoughtful, open, caring people who were as concerned for my wellbeing as I was. I had to really consider who would be in my corner.

Having the surgery was just the tip of the iceberg. What happened next was a little like finding yourself locked into the roller coaster about to leave the platform. There was no turning back, and the experience would be thrilling and confronting.

It was hard to eat anything because my stomach was sore and healing. I remembered what the doctor had instructed: "Just work on getting all your water in and staying hydrated." I took an exceptionally long time to eat 4 oz of protein, but I got it down. I had hunger pains, but they felt different. Fairly early on, I became conscious of the distinction between being thirsty and being hungry. Even today, when I take the time to listen to my body and make the right choice, it is often water over food.

Exercise was another lifestyle change that I really took on, and it was very confronting for me to find a place to work out. When I was heavy, I always felt self-conscious in gyms, sometimes even unwelcome. I walked to work and many other places in the city. I worried about gaining weight, and when I hit a plateau, I wondered, "Is the weight loss over?" I reached out to my support team for ideas. I was talking on the phone with my friend, Ellen, who suggested Gyrotonic.

At this point, I was 9 months post-op and still had over a hundred pounds to go. I found myself in a building full of professional dancers with beautiful bodies, and I was choosing this over the gym. It was not confronting at all to my body image! Showing up in my own life is a practice I've now integrated into my new life. I belonged there. I felt welcomed there. Moving your body is key to being healthy.

It is always a combination of the cards that you're dealt, and what you do with them. For me, it is more empowering to take responsibility for my part. I work to avoid body shaming myself or comparing my body to someone else's. I focus on being as healthy and fit as I can be each day. These are all choices I make throughout the day; day after day, I create the sustained success that I have enjoyed for twenty years.

The lesson I have learned, or what I have discovered about my nature, is that I set myself up for failure by striving to be perfect, to "do it right." Gaining mastery in managing my body and my health is not about being perfect. For me, it is about balance and consistency. Being conscious and continuing to distinguish behavior and triggers are key. I experimented with what was going to work for me. I have had to adjust some habits in my life, such as leaving the office at a decent hour to get in my workout. And in my career, I learned to delegate different tasks and decisions to managers who reported to me, trusting them to make decisions. I have a practice of self-reflection to determine what circumstances, actions, or behaviors are not supporting me in achieving my goals. This practice remains critical in my life today.

I have experienced life as a thin person, a fat person, and now I am back to a healthy weight. That education cannot be erased, diminished, or invalidated. I know firsthand how my size has been a distraction to my achievement and my credibility. My weight is something people had to get past before they could hear me.

Before the surgery, I was a successful businesswoman. Devoting most of my time to my career, I earned my senior vice president title in my thirties because I was lucky enough to have a manager who respected my commitment and my results rather than measuring my performance by my size. Still, I had allowed my life to become small, and I was extremely limited physically.

Today I enjoy getting on a plane and tightening the seat belt because it's too loose. I don't worry about what the seating is like in a restaurant, whether it is a booth or chairs or taller bar-type chairs. I will be comfortable.

The joy of being able to buy clothes off the rack is great, and when that garment is a size six designer suit, it's priceless. I always feel well-groomed, attractive, and professional, and even sexy, which provides greater confidence. I no longer perspire walking down the street. I can remember with delight the first time I caught myself running down the street!

I have enjoyed sleeping soundly through the night without a bathroom break. And since my surgery, I have enjoyed great times go-karting, riding bikes, and even riding a roller coaster with my nieces and nephews—two rides in a row! My joints and leg muscles do not ache. I can wear shoes for pretty people.

I've learned that success for me is about building relationships, producing results, and not about the size of my rear-end. The best is being alive and living at full throttle!

Now, in my career coaching business, I share my story with those who run into similar injustices around weight-bias, age-bias, and others. I love being fully confident in my work and I know I am an inspiration to those I work with as well as those close family members who were on this journey with me.

If you're reading my story and it inspires you at all, or maybe you ARE looking for a better-fitting career, please reach out to me! Life is too short to be doing something you aren't completely happy doing.

Whether or not you want a new career, I invite you to download my video on communication that builds authentic professional relationships. You will also be able to download my Leadership Inspiration Practices, which has 31 inspirational quotes and a corresponding skill practice to strengthen your leadership muscles. Go to www.stacygfisher.com/pivot now and get access.

Take charge of your life now! Stop waiting until the "perfect time." NOW is the perfect time.

# About Stacy Fisher

Stacy G. Fisher is a speaker and a career coach who specializes in leadership skills that propel clients to promotions. Stacy previously held leadership roles in a Fortune 40 company in currency risk management, e-commerce and organization effectiveness and development focused on strategies to enhance employee engagement, talent planning and diversity, equity and inclusion across multi-disciplined lines of business. Stacy is an enthusiastic advocate for gender equality and promoting positive body inclusivity.

# CHAPTER 10

# Lucky to Be Alive

## By Tina Palmgren

I was abandoned for 44 days at 14 months old at Mott's Children's Hospital in Ann Arbor, MI. Parents weren't allowed to stay with their children back then, and they had my brothers and a sister at home to take care of, eight hours away.

When I entered the hospital, I was still on the bottle, not eating food. The doctors decided to force me to eat, so the nurses set up a highchair on a big piece of plastic, and they said that by the third day I was eating. Because they couldn't make me eat again after my surgery, I got my bottle back! (That must be why I like bottled beer!)

I was a "blue baby," turning blue and having "spells" from lack of oxygen. I underwent testing, and after having a blue spell in the hospital, the doctors decided my surgery needed to be done sooner rather than later. They put in a heart catheter to see what was wrong with my heart.

Shortly thereafter, I developed pneumonia, which caused several more spells, but I was successfully treated with penicillin. I underwent open-heart surgery less than 3 weeks later to correct both a hole in my heart and a growth in my aortic muscle. They fixed the hole in my heart with a Teflon patch, giving me a non-stick heart!

My mom remembers all the nurses donating blood before my surgery to be sure there wouldn't be a shortage. After my surgery they would come frequently to suction out my lungs. It must have hurt, because Mom said I would try to get away even though I was all hooked up and strapped down.

My parents were finally able to take me home, scars and all. The scars became known as "my zipper."

I had several follow-up appointments, but the one that made me giggle while reading the files was from when I was two-and-a-half years old. It read, "Blood pressures were unobtainable in this youngster who thoroughly hates us." I can only imagine why I hated doctors...and it may have been where my rebel tendencies first started to show.

My mom had rubella during her pregnancy, which caused my heart issues along with the underdevelopment of my left eye. It's called a coloboma, when the retina doesn't fully develop, also called a drop-pupil. One of my very first memories is being in a hospital room with about 25 student doctors who were all looking at my eye. Being very shy and not liking doctors, I was terrified.

As a young girl, I struggled to be away from my parents, and I was extremely shy. I would go as far as pulling my dress over my head and showing my zipper, because if I couldn't see them, they couldn't see me, right?

My first overnight at a friend's house around the age of five ended in the middle of the night with me being taken back home, crying hysterically.

A few years later, I was excited to attend a church camp with two of my friends. However, when we arrived, they had overbooked the cabin, and so they separated me from the other two girls. Being super shy, I didn't get to know any of the kids in my cabin. It was an excruciatingly long week.

My family rented a cabin every summer on a lake. When I was about seven, my brother brought me out to the raft in the middle of the lake and left me there. I learned how to swim the doggy paddle that day when Mom called me in for supper. I never did rat him out; I was too scared of getting him in trouble.

My two brothers are nine and fourteen years older than me. I wanted to go with them, but as teenagers, they didn't want a younger sibling hanging out with them. For years, I felt abandoned by them not wanting me around, not realizing it was just the age difference.

My annual visit to the cardiologist when I was eight years old was memorable because they gave me a clean bill of health, saying, "Go and live a good life!" Yay, they didn't want to see me anymore!

In second grade I got my first pair of glasses. They were blue cat-eye glasses. I was so proud of them. The first time I wore them to school, all the kids laughed at me and made fun of me all day. That was the only day I wore those glasses.

I was a teacher's pet all through school. Before junior high school, I had crooked teeth, glasses, and always felt like an ugly duckling, even though I was good in school and loved to learn. Having only 44 classmates, everyone knew each other, but I hung out with my older cousins and not my classmates.

Cheerleading, golf, track, and basketball took me through high school. By my senior year I had contacts, straight teeth, and good grades, earning a two-year scholarship to the local community college. But I still struggled to make friends.

My first "real" job at the age of 16 was as a dishwasher at the golf course. At 18, I started waitressing and bartending, which taught me many skills I still use today in my business.

My junior high English teacher was a golfer, and the first time I waited on him I said, "Hi, Mr. Kelly!" He said, "Call me John." I answered, "Right, Mr. Kelly." He said, "I'm John." "Ok

Mr. Kelly!" I finally learned to call him John. He bought a golf store, and a few years ago I stopped in, and he joked, "You know, I should have never told you to call me John!"

What it taught me is that people want to be treated as themselves, not as their jobs.

I bartended my way through college and was fortunate enough not to have any student loans when I finished my BA in Accounting from Michigan State University in 1989.

My first "grown-up" job was as an accountant for a travel agency. I dove in and figured out the system, and within a week I was able to make several time- and money-saving changes to what they were previously doing. The software we used was a specialized system, and the developer learned I was an accountant. He had me test any changes he made, and that was where I started learning how to find mistakes and to figure out how to fix the problems.

After moving to the Twin Cities, I worked for a millwright contractor and developed automated systems to track our equipment out on jobs. In the first year, we were able to bill an additional $150,000 in revenue and we stopped the equipment from walking away from job sites, which was an even bigger money saver.

I continued bartending in the Twin Cities for something to do and to meet people. I met the love of my life, Pete, shortly after moving there at the age of 26. We both fell hard and fast!

Pete died after complications from a heart attack when I was 31. He left two young boys behind from his first marriage, but as a stepmom I had no rights and lost them, too. I asked God, "Why not me? I'm the one who had open heart surgery. Why am I being abandoned, again?"

I was depressed for years, never realizing it...

I moved to Stevens Point, Wisconsin for my second husband and worked several accounting jobs. The last three were for bigger corporations, and I realized I could make a difference by helping other departments to be accurate and efficient. I would find errors, dig deep to figure out where they were coming from, and then go out to that department and work with the employees to figure out the problems.

I learned it was better to ask forgiveness than to ask for permission, as permission always came with pointless meetings and wasted time, only to be told I didn't know what I was doing! Yep, out came my inner rebel: just fix it! I would get yelled at, but I just told them to give it two weeks and let me know what changes needed to be made. Every time it was, "Do you know, this is working!" You're welcome, just let me do my job!

I'm a golfer, and I was supposed to golf with my previous boss one night. His office was next to mine, and I heard him out in the hall. I asked if he had brought his clubs, but he said he was too busy and couldn't play that night. I commented back, "You're a wuss, afraid of losing to a girl!" Right then, this guy walks in that I had never seen before and introduces himself as the new president of the company! Yep, I made a great first impression, but we were on a first-name basis after that.

I remarried, but wasn't happy. After leaving my second husband, I began a journey of self-discovery that continues to this day. I've discovered my limiting belief of "I'm lucky to be alive, I don't deserve any more."

You see, growing up I frequently heard, "You're lucky to be alive!" What I didn't realize was that my subconscious owned those words. I didn't understand that I was allowing those words to hold me back: I didn't deserve to be happy, loved, abundant...

What a load of crap I allowed myself to believe for five decades. Now, I ask God, "Why did you keep me alive? What is my purpose? Who am I here to serve? What lights me up?"

Guess what? I found it right under my nose, but I kept it hidden by way of my buttoned-up professional life as an accountant and process consultant. I came alive when I bartended. My sassy, sarcastic, fun-loving side came out to play when I was serving customers. When I was slinging drinks, I stopped being the stuffy, buttoned-up businesswoman and let my social skills fly!

But I also loved the challenge of running an accurate and efficient machine. I was a pro at managing pour costs and serving up cocktails quickly without waste while keeping customers entertained and having a good time.

Once I embraced my inner passion of having fun while serving others, my business improved, too. I let go of that stuffy, buttoned-up businesswoman and now I bring the fun of numbers, yes you read that right, the fun of numbers, to my clients by creating customized plug-and-play templates to run their businesses. Besides eliminating their frustration, they get back hundreds of hours and thousands of dollars each year.

The joy I've discovered in being my sassy self while serving customers has motivated me to pursue my purpose. To put it simply, I love making your business fun and easy to run! I no longer question my existence or feel like I am wasting my time on this earth. Life is too short to dread the paperwork involved in running your business; make it fun and easy! I've forgiven myself and set myself free to embrace fun, love, and most importantly, life. I am not just lucky to be alive, but deserving to be alive and to thrive!

Looking back at my childhood, even though the doctors said I wouldn't have a normal life, my parents never held me back. They treated me as a normal kid without any physical handicaps. I ran, played sports, and did all kinds of crazy stunts. My parents told me I could do and be anything I put my mind to.

I believe this is why I am healthy to this day. My parents treated me as healthy, and so my mindset says I'm healthy.

Our words and actions matter, especially when we're talking to children. They absorb things with no filters. It's important to raise our children in a positive, encouraging environment. Don't demean or belittle them; find their strengths and encourage them to be the best they can be. What we tell our kids when they are young may stay in their subconscious minds and hold them back from living their best lives.

We've been told all our lives that we need to work on the areas where we are weak or have challenges. Think back to your report cards: you could have had all A's and one B, so what did your parents say? Was it that you needed to work on the subject with the B, or did they praise you for the A's?

I don't believe we need to strengthen our weak areas. There are others who are strong in those areas with whom we can work; they love doing the things we struggle with and don't like doing. We need to focus on our strengths and build on them to help people who are weak in our areas of expertise. As they say, it takes a village...

When you do what you love, it's not work; it's a joy, and your passion and enthusiasm will shine through. Not everyone will support you, and it's hard not to let those people keep you down who want you to stay where you are. But it's your dream, so don't let someone else tell you that it's not possible. You have the power to be anyone and anything you want. It takes work to get the negative out of your head, but it's worth it.

My challenge to you is to look inside yourself and find that story that has been holding you back for years (or, in my case, decades). It could be something you heard as a child, like mine: "You're lucky to be alive!" Or it could be something you hear all the time, like "Money is evil." Really, how can money be evil? It's a piece of paper! Seriously, look inside yourself, find the story that's holding you back, let it go, and watch your world blossom and bloom right before your eyes!

I love to read, both fiction and non-fiction. I love to learn and grow, but sometimes I just like to escape reality. I can't pick an all-time favorite book; there are just too many good ones. **I invite you to download my "Alive & Thrive" book list that has changed my life dramatically.** Most of the books I have read more than once, and I find something new within their pages every time, as I come from a new place in life each time I re-read one.

You can find my reading list on a special page I've built just for readers of this book: www.ExcelingYourBusiness.com/thrive.

I want you to not only love your life, but to thrive as the best version of your UNIQUE self. Here's to your continued learning and growth.

# About Tina Palmgren

Tina's passion is to strengthen the heartbeat of your business, solving the problems associated with running back-office systems productively, accurately, and efficiently. With a BA in Accounting, a Master's in Technology Management, 23 years' experience in accounting and finance, and 7 years' experience teaching Excel, Tina is well-positioned to help you strengthen your business's heartbeat by finding overlooked inefficiencies and errors while customizing systems to your business's needs.

# What's Next?

You may not currently be thinking about what's next for you, since we've given you so many things to get started on: discovering your transformational story, shifting your mindset, reflecting, identifying how and who your story is meant to impact, money, best practices, and so forth.

The reality is that many new writers give up and fail. Most get discouraged and feel they have nothing of value to share because they don't learn how to craft the wisdom from their life's lessons into their transformational story. Most don't seek or receive the help and mentorship that can support them and get them where they need to go next, or tell them what to do and when.

Do YOU have an obstacle or challenge that we didn't mention? Are you uncertain about how to overcome it? Do you need advice or best practices on how to tackle something in your writing, whether it's for your business or a personal story that we didn't talk about? Reach out to me, or to any of the authors, and we can help!

The *Written In Her Own Words* authors understand where you are; we get you. We also understand where you want to go and some of the struggles you'll face along the way.

I recommend you reach out to a few of the authors in this book for support, guidance, and even just to congratulate them. Sharing your transformational story is not an easy feat. It's scary to be transparent and vulnerable on the page. We know how to help you navigate around the obstacles with the least amount of damage, and then take advantage of the advice swiftly so YOU can deliver the proper impact with your unique story.

My goal is to help people like you unleash their inner writer, to have confidence and clarity in the message they are here to share with the world. I do that by being a personal guide in navigating their ongoing access to the wisdom of their life's lessons and crafting that wisdom into their transformational stories so that the people who need to find them will recognize who they are seeking.

We've hired mentors to help us get where we are. Let me and the other authors help you get where you want to go. Trust me, you will waste time and money if you don't.

Don't deny yourself the success you're seeking, and which you deserve.

Don't let your fears and doubts get in the way...just take it one step at a time.

You can do this!

# About the Author

**MARY E. KNIPPEL, BEST-SELLING AUTHOR AND
BOOK WRITING MENTOR WITH
YOURWRITINGMENTOR.COM**

**CEO OF AUTHENTIC GRACE COMMUNICATIONS**

Mary guides small business owners to write their books as a powerful driver of business growth. She helps aspiring authors to get their expertise out of their heads so that publishers and readers can find them, and they can finally make money.

If you are looking for a proven professional who uses her 35 years of experience as a journalist to ask provocative questions, uncover the heart of your message with clarity and compassion, help you craft the compelling story of your business, and put you on the path to being recognized as an expert in your field, you've come to the right place.

Mary's clients come to her when they are paralyzed about where to begin, what to say, and how to make sense of the life-changing messages they know they are here to deliver. Mary is someone who believes passionately in her clients and the importance of their messages. If you work with her, Mary will not only help you gain confidence in your writing and your ability to find the words to share your unique story, but she will also make it fun!

Mary started on her path to becoming Your Writing Mentor by writing in her own journal at the age of 11. She progressed to Humor Editor for her high school paper with visions of becoming the next Erma Bombeck. Marriage, raising a family, moving across country...twice...and breast cancer...twice...have given her plenty of journal material and the basis for her upcoming book, "The Secret Artist," part memoir and part self-help, as it chronicles the pivotal role creativity played in her recovery from breast cancer.

As a speaker, Mary calls on humor and compassion to inspire audiences to stop hiding in the shadows and living life in the safe fringe, and to step out into the spotlight to be seen. She stresses the importance of each individual, and urges clients not to live a life of regret. Mary shares the story of how her family came to her with an unusual request. Her older brother had passed away, and they wanted her to write his eulogy. She not only wrote the eulogy, but she also delivered such a heartfelt story about her brother, the entire congregation was smiling through their tears.

Speaking at the funeral solidified Mary's confidence as a speaker. Several years later (after facing down her own mortality with a breast cancer diagnosis for a second time), she fully embraced the message "you matter...your story matters," giving talks and workshops focused on helping audiences have a positive and fun writing experience. She inspires audiences to live their best lives.

What lights Mary up about this work is knowing that working together will allow your words to sparkle, shine, and compel the audience you are meant to connect with to take action because they know your core message, who you are, and what you do. You can feel confident engaging Mary to guide you and your organization to solve these problems.

What sets Mary apart from other service providers is that she has been where you are, struggling to find the words and to string them together in just the right order. She knows the triumph and that feeling of joy when you find the combination of exactly the right words to convey what you want to say, and to evoke the response you are looking for. She can help you avoid the pitfalls of an aspiring writer and the challenge of a solopreneur who falls prey to becoming overwhelmed with details and inundated with the many steps of building this new endeavor.

# Additional Resources

# Want to learn how utilizing a Book Writing Mentor can help you get the book that's inside of you out and published—finally!?

**Book a Private Discovery Call with Mary today!**

**A Book Mentor can help you:**

- Attract your ideal readers and grow your business with your successful book

- Craft compelling content that builds your audience and makes you attractive to a publisher

- Get your transformational story in your unique voice out of your head and into the world (finally)

- Walk through the 5 Building Blocks of a Book that make you the sought-after EXPERT in your field

- Avoid the 5 Big Mistakes of Book Writing (that make you invisible)

- High-touch support from a caring, compassionate mentor who knows the struggles of being vulnerable and transparent on the page

## Schedule a call today at
## www.YourWritingMentor.com/storycontact

# Interested in Becoming One of the Authors in an Upcoming Book of Ours?

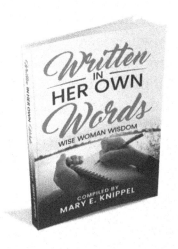

Being an author sets you apart from others in your industry and it also impresses your clients! Writing one chapter in a compilation book like this one is much faster and easier than writing an entire book yourself. It's great to have your own full-length book, but being in a compilation book or two (or three!) is a great place to start. Plus, all the authors share and promote the book too, which gives you more visibility in many markets.

**Get on our email list to be first to hear about our next compilation publishing date at www.YourWritingMentor.com/becomeanauthor**

# *Book Mary to Speak at Your Next Event!*

Any organization that wants to help their audience learn how to get their words out of their heads and onto the page would do well to book Mary as their speaker. Whether entrepreneurs and small business owners seeking to grow their businesses, or individuals looking to share their unique stories, Mary's gifted storytelling will inspire participants to discover fast and fun writing techniques.

## To Contact or Book Mary to Speak:
## Mary E. Knippel

PO Box 244

Half Moon Bay, CA  94019

650-440-5616

MentorMary@yourwritingmentor.com

www.YourWritingMentor.com/Speaking

Made in USA - North Chelmsford, MA
1339188_9780983254515
11.09.2022 0923